MEDIA
ANALYSIS
TECHNIQUES
Second Edition

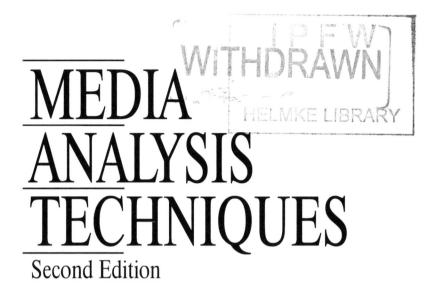

MEDIA ANALYSIS TECHNIQUES

Second Edition

Arthur Asa Berger

 SAGE Publications
International Educational and Professional Publisher
Thousand Oaks London New Delhi

For information:

 SAGE Publications, Inc.
2455 Teller Road
Thousand Oaks, California 91320
E-mail: order@sagepub.com

SAGE Publications Ltd.
6 Bonhill Street
London EC2A 4PU
United Kingdom

SAGE Publications India Pvt. Ltd.
M-32 Market
Greater Kailash I
New Delhi 110 048 India

Printed in the United States of America

Library of Congress Cataloging-in-Publication Data

Berger, Arthur Asa, 1933-
    Media analysis techniques / by Arthur Asa Berger. — 2nd ed.
      p. cm.
    Includes bibliographical references and indexes.
    ISBN 0-7619-1453-6 (acid-free paper). — ISBN 0-7619-1454-4
  (pbk.: acid-free paper)
      1. Mass media—Methodology. 2. Mass media criticism. I. Title.
    P91.B43   1998
    302.23'01—dc21   98-8876

01 02 03 04 10 9 8 7 6 5 4

Acquiring Editor:	Margaret Seawell
Editorial Assistant:	Renée Piernot
Production Editor:	Astrid Virding
Production Assistant:	Denise Santoyo
Typesetter/Designer:	Marion S. Warren
Cover Designer:	Candice Harman
Print Buyer:	Anna Chin

This book is dedicated to my colleagues in the
Broadcast & Electronic Communication Arts Department,
and to my students.

Contents

PART I. Techniques of Interpretation

PART II. Applications

Preface to the Second Edition

The first edition of *Media Analysis Techniques* appeared in 1982, and a revised edition appeared in 1991. I originally wrote the book because I had a notion that it would be a good idea to bring together material that would enable students to make their own analyses of films, television programs, advertisements, MTV—whatever. Fortunately, the editors at Sage Publications agreed, and the book was published. It is gratifying for me to know that many students have found the book useful.

WHY BOTHER LEARNING ABOUT CRITICISM?

Students sometimes ask me why they should learn about media analysis when they could be taking "practical" studio or production courses. I explain to them that criticism and creativity are two sides of the same coin. Creative people (directors, artists, musicians, performers, and so on) must be analytic about what they do; they need to understand why their work succeeds when it does, and how to avoid repeating their mistakes.

If you are a creative artist and you don't know what you're doing, everything you do is, in effect, an accident. That's why artists study art history and film students study film history and film theory. It's the theory that drives the practice—in the arts and in industry as well.

For many years, my department held a large annual media conference, to which we invited people from the broadcasting media and related areas to give presentations to our students. It was remarkable how many of our graduates, invited back to speak because of their success in the broadcasting industry, mentioned the shocks they had when they went to work and discovered—to their astonishment—that the media analysis course turned out to be one of the three most important courses they had taken. (The other two, incidentally, were courses in aesthetics and research. You students who want to take only studio or production courses—read this and weep!) Consistently, our former students who have gone to work in broadcasting and related industries have told us that the knowledge they gained in the media analysis course and several other theory courses was the most useful part of their education. Anyone can be taught to operate a camera (or other device). It's what you do with that camera that counts.

WHAT'S NEW IN THIS EDITION?

For this new edition of *Media Analysis Techniques*, I have updated and otherwise enhanced the discussions of methodology in Part I, and I have written a new chapter on advertising for Part II. Also, a number of professors who use or have used the book in the first and revised editions made some suggestions that were very helpful, and I am deeply grateful to these anonymous reviewers. As a result of their suggestions, I have made some further additions to the book: a glossary of some of the terms used; study questions and topics for discussion for each chapter; a new chapter devoted to learning games, exercises, and activities; and a number of new illustrations to give the book more visual appeal. I hope that as a result of these revisions, readers will find this edition even more helpful and useful than earlier ones.

The original edition of *Media Analysis Techniques* has been translated into Italian, Chinese, and Korean (it may be in other languages as well, but if so, I don't know about them—I didn't know about the Chinese version until I was invited to a conference in Taiwan). The person who wrote the preface for the Italian edition said that it is a useful guide for high school students. I have also met professors who have told me they've used it in graduate seminars. And, of course, it has been used at many other levels as well.

I hope this new edition of *Media Analysis Techniques* will help you, my readers, to gain enough understanding of semiotic theory, psychoanalytic theory, Marxist theory, and sociological theory that you can become your own media analysts and critics. If this happens, I will have accomplished my purpose.

Preface to the Revised Edition

It is a great pleasure for me to write a preface to the revised edition of this book. *Media Analysis Techniques* was published in 1982, so it is almost ten years between editions. Ten years and eleven printings. And an Italian version, *Tecniche di analisi dei mass media*, published by ERI/Edizioni Rai Radiotelevisione Italiana, as well.

I think *Media Analysis Techniques* has achieved its modest success because it empowers its readers. There are, I believe, two fundamental ways to teach media criticism. One way is ask students to read critical essays and discuss the content of these essays . . . and, perhaps, deal with the methodology employed by the writers. The other way is to focus on methods: teach students methodologies and give the students an opportunity to apply the methodologies to television programs, films, advertisements, and various other texts. My book takes the methodological approach, though in the second half of the book I offer a number of essays which show how the four techniques discussed in the first part of the book can be applied.

Popular culture changes so rapidly that just about any film or television series you deal with becomes part of what my students see as "ancient history." Therefore, I chose topics for the applications section that won't get outdated: a classic detective story (which was made into a very fine film), football (with a focus on how it is presented on television), magazine advertising, and all-news radio.

I have made a moderate number of additions to the chapters. For the most part I have added new concepts to the methodology chapters and amplified my discussion of certain topics that I felt needed more elaboration. The subjects I deal with in the first half of the book, semiology/semiotics, psychoanalytic criticism, Marxist theory, and sociological criticism, are all enormously complex and each have been the subjects of endless numbers of articles and books. (*Media Analysis Techniques* is a thin book that could easily become a very fat book . . . or four very fat books.) What I have tried to do, in each discussion, is focus upon concepts that help us understand texts and the mass media. I chose these four methodologies because I think they are of paramount importance, but there are many other approaches that could have been taken. I discuss this subject in the epilogue of the book.

I hope that this edition of *Media Analysis Techniques* helps readers better understand the four methodologies discussed and that this little book will help readers gain enough understanding of the techniques discussed so they can become their own media analysts. I have added some new sources to the bibliographies at the end of each chapter and have also added an index.

Preface to the First Edition

Imagine, if you will, a room in which four people are sitting, watching the episode of *Dallas* in which J.R. Ewing is shot. The four people are television critics, each for one of the following magazines: *Marxist Critical Studies of Media*, *Psychoanalysis and the Public Arts*, *Sign: Semiological Inquiries Into Popular Culture*, and *Media and Society*. None of these magazines exists, as far as I know, but publications like them do.

After watching the program, each critic writes a review suitable for his or her publication. The Marxist critic dwells on the degradation of the characters and shows how each is alienated, reflecting the horrors of bourgeois capitalist societies in general and America in particular. *Dallas*, then, is an unwitting exposé of the moral degeneracy and corruption found in all bourgeois capitalist societies. The psychoanalytically oriented critic explains that *Dallas* is *really* about the Oedipal problems of J.R., which are unresolved, and his sibling rivalry with Bobby. J.R.'s behavior is best explained, then, using psychoanalytic concepts. J.R. has no superego or conscience and this is tied, ultimately, to his relationship with his mother. The semiological critic would focus attention on how meaning is generated in the program—on the significance of Southfork and the Ewing tower, J.R.'s overdrawn facial expressions, the spatiality of the sets, and everything else that is done to give viewers the ideas and feelings that the writers, actors, and directors want the audience to have. And the sociological critic would focus on the various roles the characters have, the fact that certain social groupings are underrepresented (or not represented) in the program, and the different gratifications that members of the audience get from watching the program.

After reading this book you should be able to write all four of these types of reviews. The first section of the book is made up of chapters that introduce semiological, psychoanalytic (Freudian), Marxist, and sociological thought. These chapters should be read as "primers" that discuss some of the more important concepts in each domain. An annotated bibliography is provided at the end of each of these chapters, to assist the reader in finding useful books in each area.

The second section of the book consists of essays that demonstrate how the various perspectives might be applied to the public arts. Thus you will find chapters on *Murder on the Orient Express*, fashion and cosmetic advertising in *Vogue*, football, and all-news radio stations that use the techniques explained in the first part of the book.

I hope you will find this volume informative and entertaining, and that it will help you to see the public arts and popular culture in new and interesting ways.

Acknowledgments

My thanks to: Groucho Marx, Karl Marx, Sigmund Freud, Fustel de Coulanges, Roland Barthes, Umberto Eco, Agostino Lombardo, Giuseppe Gadda-Conti, Jean-Marie Benoist, George Gerbner, Dave Noble, Marshall McLuhan, Michael Real, Vladimir Propp, Ernest Dichter, Claude Lévi-Strauss, William Fry, Jr., Bronislaw Malinowski, Ferdinand de Saussure, Johan Huizinga, Joe Meeker, Irving Louis Horowitz, Jason Berger, Jonathan Culler, Stanley Milgram, Mircea Eliade, John Cawelti, Cecilia Bartholomew, Henri Lefebvre, Elihu Katz, Daniel Dayan, Mike Noll, Peter Clarke, Ev Dennis, Howard and Barbara Ginsberg, Isaac Silberman, Ron Compesi, Howard Rheingold, Conrad Kottak, Asa Briggs, Tony Fellow, Tom Inge, Jeremy Klein, Raphael Patai, Mary Douglas, Bruno Bettelheim, David Manning White, Orrin Klapp, Warren Bennis, Tom and Bella Clougher, Alan Dundes, Brom Weber, Mulford Q. Sibley, Lauri Honko, Jean Guenot, Randy Harrison, Claude Cossette, and Stan Lee. My chapter on semiological/semiotic analysis (Chapter 1) appeared, in slightly modified form, in *Understanding Television: Essays on Television as a Social and Cultural Force*, edited by Richard P. Adler. Special thanks to Aaron Wildavsky, for his sage counsel, and to F. Gerald Kline, for his editorial advice.

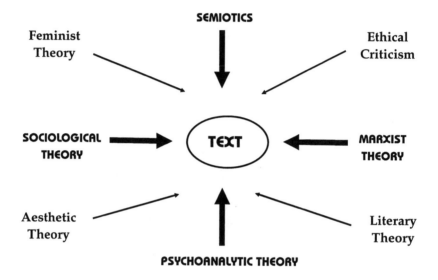

Methods of Interpreting a Text

PART I

Techniques of Interpretation

Semiology is the term for the science of signs explicated by the Swiss linguist Ferdinand de Saussure. A different science of signs, semiotics, was first elaborated by the American philosopher Charles Sanders Peirce. Semiotics is the term now generally used to refer to both systems. Both are concerned with how meaning is generated in "texts" (films, television programs, and other works of art). In this chapter, after a discussion of the most essential semiotic concepts and some related concerns, semiotic concepts are applied to an episode of a television program. Codes, formulas, and the "language" of television are then addressed.

CHAPTER 1

Semiotic Analysis

I face this assignment—explaining semiotics and showing how it can be applied to television and popular culture to those who know little or nothing about the subject—with a certain amount of apprehension. I'm not sure whether semiotics is a subject, a movement, a philosophy, or a cultlike religion. I do know that there is a large and rapidly expanding literature on the subject and that many of the writings of semioticians are difficult and highly technical.

So my mission, if not impossible, is quite challenging—not only am I to explain the fundamental notions or elements of semiotics, I am also to apply them to television and television productions as well as to popular culture in general. It is a large undertaking, but I think it can be done.

The price I must pay involves a certain amount of simplification and narrowness of focus. I am going to explain the basic principles of semiotics and discuss some sample applications. I hope that after reading this chapter and the annotated bibliography provided, those interested in semiotics will probe more deeply into it at their own convenience.

A BRIEF HISTORY OF THE SUBJECT

Although interest in signs and the way they communicate has a long history (medieval philosophers, John Locke, and others have shown interest), modern semiotic analysis can be said to have begun with two men—Swiss linguist Ferdinand de Saussure (1857-1913) and American philosopher Charles Sanders Peirce (1839-1914). (Peirce called his system *semiotics,* and that has become the dominant term used for the science of signs. Saussure's semiology differs from Peirce's semiotics in some respects, but as both are concerned with signs, I will treat the two as more or less the same in this chapter.)

Saussure's book *A Course in General Linguistics,* first published posthumously in 1915, suggests the possibility of semiotic analysis. It deals with many of the concepts that can be applied to signs and that are explicated in this chapter. Saussure's division of the sign into two components, the signifier, or "sound-image," and the signified, or "concept," and his suggestion that the relationship between signifiers and signified is arbitrary were of crucial importance for the development of semiotics. Peirce, on the other hand, focused on three aspects of signs— their iconic, indexical, and symbolic dimensions (see Table 1.1).

From these two points of departure a movement was born, and semiotic analysis has spread all over the globe. Important work was done in Prague and Russia early in the 20th century, and semiotics is now well established in France and Italy (where Roland Barthes, Umberto Eco, and many others have done important theoretical as well as applied work). There are also outposts of progress in England, the United States, and many other countries.

Semiotics has been applied, with interesting results, to film, theater, medicine, architecture, zoology, and a host of other areas that involve or are concerned with communication and the transfer of information. In fact, some semioticians, perhaps carried away, suggest that *everything* can be analyzed semiotically; they see semiotics as the queen of the interpretive sciences, the key that unlocks the meanings of all things great and small.

Peirce argued that interpreters have to supply part of the meanings of signs. He wrote that a sign "is something which stands to somebody for something in some respect or capacity" (quoted in Zeman, 1977, p. 24). This is different from Saussure's ideas about how signs function. Peirce considered semiotics important because, as he put it, "this universe is perfused with signs, if it is not composed exclusively of signs." Whatever we do can be seen as a message, or as Peirce would put it, a sign. If everything in the universe is a sign, semiotics becomes

TABLE 1.1 Three Aspects of Signs

	Icon	*Index*	*Symbol*
Signify by	resemblance	causal connections	conventions
Examples	pictures	statues	smoke/fire
Process	can see	can figure out	must learn

extremely important, if not all-important (a view that semioticians support wholeheartedly).

Whether this is the case is questionable, but without doubt semiotics has been used by all kinds of people in interesting ways. It has only recently been taken seriously in the United States, however, and is still not widely used or taught here. There are several reasons for this. First, Americans tend to be pragmatic and down-to-earth; we do not generally find abstruse, theoretical, and formalistic methodologies congenial. Also, a kind of international cultural lag exists; it takes a while for movements that are important in the European intellectual scene to become accepted, let alone popular, in the United States. It was the French who "discovered" Faulkner and film (as a significant art form), and, though Peirce did important work on semiotics in the United States, Americans had to wait for semiotic analysis to evolve and mature in Europe before it caught our attention.

THE PROBLEM OF MEANING

In what follows, you are going to be learning a new language, in the form of a number of concepts that will enable you to look at films, television programs, fashion, foods—almost anything—in ways somewhat different from the manner in which you may be used to looking at these things. The basic concern of this discussion is *how meaning is generated and conveyed*, with particular reference to the television programs we will be examining (which will be referred to here as *texts*).

But how is meaning generated? The essential breakthrough of semiotics is that it takes linguistics as a model and applies linguistic concepts to other phenomena—texts—and not just to language itself. In fact, semioticians treat texts as being like languages, in that relationships are all-important, and not things per se. To quote Jonathan Culler (1976):

> The notion that linguistics might be useful in studying other cultural phenomena is based on two fundamental insights: first, that social and cultural phenomena are not simply material objects or events but objects or events with meaning, and hence signs; and second, that they do not have essences but are defined by a network of relations. (p. 4)

Signs and relations—these are two of the key notions of semiotic analysis. A text such as *Star Trek* can be thought of as a system of signs, and the meaning in the program stems from the signs and from the system that ties the signs together. This system is generally not obvious and must be elicited from the text.

In semiotic analysis, an arbitrary and temporary separation is made between content and form, and attention is focused on the system of signs that makes up a text. Thus a meal, to stray from television for a moment, is not seen as steak, salad, baked potato, and apple pie, but rather as a sign system conveying meanings related to matters such as status, taste, sophistication, and nationality.

Perhaps it would be useful to quote one of the founding fathers of semiotics, Ferdinand de Saussure (1966):

> Language is a system of signs that express ideas, and is therefore comparable to a system of writing, the alphabet of deaf-mutes, symbolic rites, polite formulas, military signals, etc. But it is the most important of all these systems.
>
> *A science that studies the life of signs within society* is conceivable; it would be a part of social psychology and consequently of general psychology; I shall call it *semiology* (from Greek *semeion* "sign"). Semiology would show what constitutes signs, what laws govern them. Since the science does not yet exist, no one can say what it would be; but it has a right to existence, a place staked out in advance. (p. 16)

This is the charter statement of semiotics, a statement that opens the study of media to us, for not only can we study symbolic rites and military signals, we can also study commercials, soap operas, situation comedies, and almost anything else as "sign systems."

Saussure offered another crucial insight that is relevant here: that concepts have meaning because of relations, and the basic relationship is oppositional. Thus "rich" doesn't mean anything unless there is "poor," or "happy" unless there is "sad." "Concepts are purely differential and defined not by their positive content but negatively by their relations with the other terms of the system" (Saussure, 1966, p. 117). It is not "content" that determines meaning, but "relations" in some kind of a system. The "most precise characteristic" of these concepts "is in being what the others are not" (p. 117). We can see this readily enough in language, but it also holds for texts. Nothing has meaning in itself!

One thing we must remember when thinking about oppositions is that the opposing concepts must be related in some way. There is always some topic (not always mentioned) that connects them. For example: rich/WEALTH/poor or happy/MENTAL STATE/sad. I wrote an article a number of years ago in which I discussed blue jeans and what I called the "denimization" phenomenon and contrasted it with the wearing of fancy clothes. Some of the differences are listed below, with the topics addressed appearing in capital letters:

DENIM		*FANCY CLOTHES*
cheap	COST	expensive
rough	TEXTURE	smooth
mass-produced	FABRICATION	hand-made
department stores	PLACE BOUGHT	boutiques

If you think of a pair of terms you believe are oppositional, but can find no subject that both relate to, there is probably something wrong with the pairing of those terms.

So where are we now? I have suggested that semiotic analysis is concerned with meaning in texts and that meaning stems from relationships—in particular, the relationship among signs. But what, exactly, is a sign?

SIGNS

A sign, according to Saussure (1966), is a combination of a concept and a sound-image, a combination that cannot be separated. But because

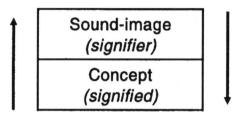

Figure 1.1. Saussure's Diagram of a Sign

Saussure does not find these terms quite satisfactory, he modifies them slightly:

> I propose to retain the word sign [*signe*] to designate the whole and to replace concept and sound-image respectively by *signified* [*signifié*] and *signifier* [*signifiant*]; the last two terms have the advantage of indicating the opposition that separates them from each other and from the whole of which they are parts. (p. 67)

The relationship between the signifier and signified—and this is crucial—is *arbitrary*, unmotivated, unnatural. There is no logical connection between a word and a concept or a signifier and signified, a point that makes finding meaning in texts interesting and problematic.

Saussure uses trees as an example. He offers a diagram of the sign in general (see Figure 1.1) and then of the *sign* tree (Figure 1.2). The difference between a sign and a symbol, Saussure suggests, is that a symbol has a signifier that is never wholly arbitrary:

> One characteristic of the symbol is that it is never wholly arbitrary; it is not empty, for there is a rudiment of a natural bond between the signifier and signified. The symbol of justice, a pair of scales, could not be replaced by just another symbol, such as a chariot. (p. 68)

We can now start looking at texts differently and can start thinking about how it is that signifiers generate meaning. How do signifiers generate meaning? And how is it that we know these meanings? If the relationship between signifier and signified is arbitrary, the meanings that signifiers hold must be learned somehow, which implies that there

Figure 1.2. Saussure's Diagram of a Sign and Symbol "Tree"

are certain structured associations, or *codes,* that we pick up that help us interpret signs. (I will deal with this subject in more detail shortly.)

Let's look at the television program *Star Trek* in terms of its signifiers and what is signified. Anyone who has seen the program knows that it is a space adventure/science fiction series. We know this because we are told so at the beginning of each episode, when the captain's voice-over describes the mission of the starship *Enterprise*—to explore new worlds and seek out new civilizations, "to boldly go where no man has gone before." We can say that science fiction adventure is the general "signified" and that a number of "signifiers" show this, including spaceships, futuristic uniforms, ray guns, advanced computer technology, extraterrestrials with strange powers (such as Mr. Spock, whose pointy ears signify that he is only partly human), and magic/science.

It is precisely because the program is so rich in signifiers that legions of "Trekkers" are able to hold conventions, wear costumes, sell "phasers," and so on. When you have appropriated the signifiers, you have captured, so to speak, the signified. This, I might point out, is how many commercials work. People purchase the "right" products and assume (or hope) that these products will signify a certain social class, status, lifestyle, or what you will.

All of this is based on associations we learn and then carry around with us. Anyone who communicates uses associations between signifiers and signifieds all the time. Because in real life the relationships are arbitrary and change rapidly, one must be on one's toes all the time. Signifiers can become dated and change their significance all too quickly. In a sense, then, we are all practicing semioticians who pay a great deal of attention to signs—signifiers and signifieds—even though we may never have heard these terms before.

SIGN	
signifier Sound-image	*signified* Concept

Figure 1.3.

Many of us have followed the adventures of a detective who is (like all classical detectives) a first-class semiotician—though we were unaware of this because we didn't know about the existence of semiotics. I am talking about Sherlock Holmes. Inevitably, in a Sherlock Holmes mystery story, there is some situation that arises that puzzles everyone, which Holmes then "solves." He does this by reading signs that others have ignored or have believed to be trivial or inconsequential. In one story, "The Blue Carbuncle," Watson finds Holmes examining a hat that had been brought to him by a policeman. Watson describes the hat: It is old, its lining is discolored, and it is cracked, very dusty, and spotted in places. Holmes asks Watson what he can deduce from the hat about its wearer. Watson examines the hat and says that he can deduce nothing. Holmes then proceeds to describe, in remarkable detail, what the man who owned the hat is like: He is highly intellectual, has had a decline in fortune, his wife no longer loves him, he is sedentary, and he probably doesn't have gas in his house. Watson exclaims, "You are certainly joking, Holmes." Holmes then shows Watson how he reached his conclusions. He examined the hat, noticed certain things about it (signifiers), and proceeded from there (described the implied signifieds):

Signifiers	*Signifieds*
cubic capacity of hat (large brain)	Man is intellectual.
good quality hat, but 3 years old	Man hasn't a new hat, suggesting decline in fortune.
hat not brushed in weeks	Man's wife no longer loves him.
dust on hat is brown house dust	Man seldom goes out.
wax stains from candles on hat	No gas in house.

Holmes explains Watson's mistake: "You fail . . . to reason from what you see. You are too timid in drawing your inferences." Watson had said that he saw nothing in the hat. What he did was to fail to recognize the signifiers he found for what they were. This failure is common in readers of detective novels, who pass over vital information, not recognizing it for what it is. Some semioticians are, on the other hand, not timid enough in drawing their inferences, but that is another matter. The meanings in signs, and in texts (which can be looked upon as collections of signs), are not always (or even often) evident; they have to be elicited. And too many people are like Watson, I would suggest— not bold enough in drawing inferences.

SIGNS AND TRUTH

Umberto Eco (1976), a distinguished Italian semiotician, has suggested that if signs can be used to tell the truth, they can also be used to lie:

> Semiotics is concerned with everything that can be taken as a sign. A sign is everything which can be taken as significantly substituting for something else. This something else does not necessarily have to exist or to actually be somewhere at the moment in which a sign stands for it. Thus semiotics is in principle the discipline studying everything which can be used in order to lie. If something cannot be used to tell a lie, conversely it cannot be used to tell the truth; it cannot be used "to tell" at all. I think that the definition of a "theory of the lie" should be taken as a pretty comprehensive program for a general semiotics. (p. 7)

Let us consider some ways in which we can (and do) lie—or, to be kinder, mislead others with signs:

Area	Misleading Signs
wigs	bald person or person with different hair color
elevator shoes	short person made taller
dyed hair	brunettes become blondes; blondes become redheads, and so on
falsies	women with small breasts seem to have big ones
impostors	pretend to be doctors, lawyers, or whatever
impersonation	pretend to be someone else, steal "identity"
malingering	pretend to be ill
theater	pretend to have feelings, beliefs, and the like
food	imitation crab, shrimp, lobster, and so on
words	white lies told so as not to hurt people

We live in a world full of signs that lie and mislead, and many of us spend a good deal of effort trying to determine whether or not we are being conned. Much of this lying with signs is relatively harmless (the blondes who are naturally brunettes), but in some cases (the truck driver who pretends to be a doctor) it can be very dangerous. Eco's point is an important one: If signs can be used to communicate, they can be used to communicate lies.

LANGUAGE AND SPEAKING

Earlier, I suggested that texts (such as films, television programs, and commercials) are "like languages," and that the rules of linguistics can be applied to them. What a language does is enable the communication of information, feelings, ideas, and the like by establishing systems and rules that people learn. And just as there is grammar for writing and speaking, there are grammars for various kinds of texts—and for different media.

Saussure makes a distinction that is useful here—between *language* and *speaking*. Language is a social institution, made up of rules and conventions that have been systematized, that enables us to speak (or, more broadly, to communicate). Each person "speaks" in his or her own manner, but this speaking is based on the language and rules that everyone learns. A television program such as *Star Trek*—and I must point out that most of what I'm discussing here involves narratives—can be looked upon as speech that is intelligible to its audience because the audience knows the language. That is, we know the signs and what they signify; we know the conventions of the genre, or what is acceptable and unacceptable. We know the codes!

Sometimes there is confusion, and the code of the creator of a program isn't the code of the members of the audience. In such cases there is bad communication. What makes things complicated is the fact that, generally speaking, people are not consciously aware of the rules and codes and cannot articulate them, though they respond to them. A scene in a film or TV program that is meant to be sad but occasions laughter is an example of this kind of mix-up.

It is obvious, then, that people are "speaking" all the time, even when they aren't saying anything verbally. Hairstyles, eyeglasses, clothes, facial expressions, posture, gestures, and many other things communicate or "speak" (that is, signify continually) to those who are sensitive to such things and who are mindful of signs and signifiers. Maya Pines (1982) has offered this explanation of semiotics:

> Everything we do sends messages about us in a variety of codes, semiologists contend. We are also on the receiving end of innumerable messages encoded in music, gestures, foods, rituals, books, movies, or advertisements. Yet we seldom realize that we have received such messages, and would have trouble explaining the rules under which they operate.

What semiotics does, Pines adds, is teach us how to decipher these rules and "bring them to consciousness." I have described the messages we give and receive as being similar to "speech." Speech always implies, as Saussure (1966) tells us, an established system, though this system is also evolving continually.

Let me offer a brief summary of what we have covered thus far concerning semiotics:

1. Semiotics is concerned with how *meaning* is created and conveyed in texts and, in particular, in narratives (or stories).
2. The focus of semiotics is the *signs* found in texts. Signs are understood to be combinations of *signifiers* and *signifieds.*
3. Because nothing has meaning in itself, the *relationships* that exist among signs are crucial. An analogy can be made with words and grammar: It is the ways in which words are combined that determine what they mean. *Language* is a social institution that tells how words are to be used; *speaking* is an individual act based on language.
4. *Texts* can be looked upon as being similar to speech and as implying grammars or languages that make the texts meaningful. There are codes and conventions that make the signs in a narrative understandable and that also shape the actions.

CONNOTATION AND DENOTATION

The word *connotation* comes from the Latin *connotare,* "to mark along with," and refers to the cultural meanings that become attached to words (and other forms of communication). A word's connotations

involve the symbolic, historic, and emotional matters connected to it.
In his book *Mythologies* (1972), Roland Barthes, a distinguished French
semiotician, addresses the cultural connotations of many aspects of
French daily life, such as steak and *frites*, detergents, Citroen automobiles, and wrestling. His purpose, he says, is to take the world of
"what-goes-without-saying" and show this world's connotations and,
by extension, its ideological foundations.

Denotation, on the other hand, refers to the literal or explicit meanings of words and other phenomena. For example, *Barbie Doll* denotes
a toy doll, first marketed in 1959, that was originally 11.5 inches high,
had measurements of 5.25 inches at the bust, 3.0 inches at the waist, and
4.25 inches at the hips. The connotations of *Barbie Doll*, in contrast, are
the subject of some controversy. Some scholars have suggested that
the arrival of the Barbie Doll signified the end of motherhood as a
dominant role for women and the importance of consumer culture,
because Barbie is a consumer who spends her time buying clothes and
having relationships with Ken and other dolls. The Barbie Doll doesn't
prepare little girls for the traditional role of motherhood in the way
other kinds of dolls do—allowing them to imitate their mothers in
caring for their "children." The lists in Table 1.2 contrast connotation
and denotation.

A great deal of media analysis involves discovering the connotations of objects and symbolic phenomena and of the actions and dialogue of the characters in texts—that is, the meanings these may have
for audiences—and tying these meanings to social, cultural, ideological,
and other concerns.

THE SYNCHRONIC AND THE DIACHRONIC

The distinction between the synchronic and the diachronic is yet another legacy from Saussure. As he uses the terms, *synchronic* means
analytic and *diachronic* means historical, so a synchronic study of a text
looks at the relationships that exist among its elements and a diachronic
study looks at the way the narrative evolves. Another way of putting
this is that in conducting a synchronic analysis of a text, one looks for
the pattern of paired oppositions buried in the text (the paradigmatic

TABLE 1.2 Comparison of Connotation and Denotation

Connotation	Denotation
figurative	literal
signified(s)	signifier(s)
inferred	obvious
suggests meanings	describes
realm of myth	realm of existence

structure), whereas in doing diachronic analysis, one focuses upon the chain of events (the syntagmatic structure) that forms the narrative.

Saussure (1966) makes a distinction between static (synchronic) linguistics and evolutionary (diachronic) linguistics:

> All sciences would profit by indicating more precisely the coordinates along which their subject matter is aligned. Everywhere distinctions should be made . . . between (1) *the axis of simultaneity* . . . , which stands for the relations of coexisting things and from which the intervention of time is excluded; and (2) *the axis of successions* . . . , on which only one thing can be considered at a time but upon which are located all the things on the first axis together with their changes. (pp. 79-80)

To explain the differences between these two perspectives, Saussure suggests that the reader imagine a plant. If one makes a longitudinal cut in the stem of a plant, one sees the fibers that make up the plant, but if one makes a cross-sectional cut, one can see the plant's fibers in relationship to each another.

Table 1.3 contrasts synchronic analysis and diachronic analysis. For example, a researcher might focus on the way video games have evolved (thus using a diachronic perspective), or might compare the most important video games being played at a particular moment in time (thus using a synchronic perspective). Or the researcher could first utilize a diachronic perspective, to establish context, and then do a synchronic analysis, focusing on some important games. Claude Lévi-Strauss and Vladimir Propp are mentioned in the table as exemplars of

TABLE 1.3 Elements of Synchronic Analysis and Diachronic Analysis

Synchronic	Diachronic
simultaneity	succession
static	evolutionary
instant in time	historical perspective
relations in a system	relations in time
analysis the focus	development the focus
paradigmatic	syntagmatic
Lévi-Strauss	Propp

these two styles of analysis. Their ideas will be explained in the sections that follow.

SYNTAGMATIC ANALYSIS

A syntagm is a chain, and in syntagmatic analysis, a text is examined as a sequence of events that forms some kind of narrative. In this section I will discuss the ideas of Vladimir Propp, a Russian folklorist who wrote a pioneering book in 1928 titled *Morphology of the Folktale.* Morphology is the study of forms—that is, the component parts of something and their relationships to each other and to the whole.

Propp (1928/1968), whose work involved a group of fairy tales, has described his method as follows:

> We are undertaking a comparison of the themes of these tales. For the sake of comparison we shall separate the component parts of fairy tales by special methods; and then, we shall make a comparison of the tales according to their components. The result will be a morphology (i.e., a description of the tale according to its component parts and the relationship of these components to each other and to the whole). (p. 19)

Propp refers to the essential or basic narrative unit in his study as a "function" (see pp. 21-23):

Function is understood as an act of a character, defined from the point of view of its significance for the course of the action.

Propp's observations may be briefly formulated in the following manner:

1. Functions of characters serve as stable, constant elements in a tale, independent of how and by whom they are fulfilled. They constitute the fundamental components of a tale.
2. The number of functions known to the fairy tale is limited.
3. The sequence of functions is always identical.
4. All fairy tales are of one type in regard to their structure.

Propp's work has great significance for this discussion, for we can adopt and adapt his ideas to films, television stories, comics, and all kinds of other narratives. Whether or not Propp was correct in all his assertions is not of great importance for our purposes. His concept of functions can be applied to all kinds of texts with interesting results.

For each of his functions, Propp gives a summary of its essence, an abbreviated definition, and a conventional sign or designation. Some of the functions are rather complicated and have numerous subcategories, all of which fulfill the same task. Propp's (1928/1968) description of his first function is quoted below, so that you can see what a simple one is like and how he develops each (the numbers in parentheses refer to specific fairy tales that Propp studied):

I. ONE OF THE MEMBERS OF A FAMILY ABSENTS HIMSELF FROM HOME. (Definition: *absentation*. Designation: β.)

1. *The person absenting himself can be a member of the older generation* (β1). Parents leave for work (113). "The prince had to go on a distant journey, leaving his wife to the care of strangers" (265). "Once, he (a merchant) went away to foreign lands" (17). Usual forms of absentation: going to work, to the forest, to trade, to war, "on business."
2. *An intensified form of absentation is represented by the death of parents* (β2).
3. *Sometimes members of the younger generation absent themselves* (β3). They go visiting (101), fishing (108), for a walk (137), out to gather berries (244). (p. 26)

TABLE 1.4 Propp's Functions

α	*Initial situation*	Members of family or hero introduced.
β	*Absentation*	One of the members of the family absents himself from home.
γ	*Interdiction*	An interdiction is addressed to the hero.
δ	*Violation*	An interdiction is violated.
ε	*Reconnaissance*	The villain makes an attempt at reconnaissance.
η	*Delivery*	The villain receives information about his victim.
ζ	*Trickery*	The villain attempts to deceive his victim.
θ	*Complicity*	The victim submits to deception, unwittingly helps his enemy.
A	*Villainy*	The villain causes harm or injury to a member of a family.
a	*Lack*	One member of a family lacks something or wants something.
B	*Mediation*	Misfortune is made known, hero is dispatched.
C	*Counteraction*	Seekers agree to decide on counteraction.
↑	*Departure*	The hero leaves home.
D	*1st function of donor*	Hero is tested, receives magical agent or helper.
E	*Hero's reaction*	Hero reacts to actions of the future donor.
F	*Receipt of magic agent*	Hero acquires the use of a magical agent.
G	*Spatial transference*	Hero led to object of search.
H	*Struggle*	Hero and villain join in direct combat.
J	*Branding*	Hero is branded.
I	*Victory*	Villain is defeated.
K	*Liquidation*	Initial misfortune or lack is liquidated.

This is one of the briefer descriptions Propp provides for his functions; for instance, function 8 (about a villain doing harm or injury to a member of a family) has 19 subcategories.

Even though you do not know all the subcategories of each function, you can still use Propp's 31 functions to make syntagmatic analyses of selected texts (Table 1.4 displays a simplified and slightly modified list of these functions and gives a brief description of each). What will become obvious to you as you use these functions is the degree to which many contemporary stories contain many of Propp's functions. His definition of the hero as "that character who either directly suffers from the action of the villain . . . or who agrees to liquidate the misfor-

TABLE 1.4 Continued

↓	*Return*	The hero returns.
Pr	*Pursuit*	A chase: The hero is pursued.
Rs	*Rescue*	Rescue of hero from pursuit.
O	*Unrecognized arrival*	The hero, unrecognized, arrives home or in another country.
L	*Unfounded claims*	A false hero presents unfounded claims.
M	*Difficult task*	A difficult task is proposed to the hero.
N	*Solution*	The task is resolved.
Q	*Recognition*	The hero is recognized.
Ex	*Exposure*	The false hero or villain is exposed.
T	*Transfiguration*	The hero is given a new appearance.
U	*Punishment*	The villain is punished.
W	*Wedding*	The hero is married and ascends the throne.

There are seven dramatis personae in Propp's scheme:

1	Villain	Fights with hero.
2	Donor	Provides hero with magical agent.
3	Helper	Aids hero in solving difficult tasks, etc.
4	Princess	Sought-for person.
	Her father	Assigns difficult tasks.
5	Dispatcher	Sends hero on his mission.
6	Hero	Searches for something or fights with villain.
7	False hero	Claims to be hero but is unmasked.

tune or lack of another person" is also worth considering (p. 50). Heroes also, Propp tells us, are supplied with magical agents or helpers that they make use of in difficult situations.

I will now apply Propp's functions to an episode of the television program *The Prisoner* to show how Propp's work can be used to help uncover the morphology of a narrative text. *The Prisoner* is a remarkable "existential" television series first broadcast a number of years ago and today regarded by many as a classic. It is about a man who, having resigned from some mysterious (apparently espionage) organization, has been abducted and is being held against his will in "the Village," a strange resortlike place on an island, where everyone is called by a number rather than by name. The hero is locked into battles with various adversaries, each called Number Two, in the 17 episodes of the series. At the end of the series, the prisoner (Number Six) escapes from the Village, which he destroys, and returns to his apartment in London.

The first episode of *The Prisoner* is titled "Arrival." It opens with a scene in which the hero, unnamed, is shown resigning. He is in an office with some officials; he pounds the table and leaves. He returns to his apartment and begins to pack, but as he does he is gassed and passes out. He awakes in the Village, a totalitarian society where everyone has numbers instead of names; he is told that he is Number Six. The prisoner is pitted against Number Two, who wishes to find out why Six resigned. Six tries to escape by running along the seashore, but is "captured" by a huge and terrifying rubber sphere, Rover, that is kept beneath the sea and is controlled by Number Two. Six is sent to the Village hospital, where he finds himself sharing a room with an old friend, also a spy. While Six is being examined by a doctor, there is a commotion outside the exam room. Six rushes back to his room and is told that his friend has committed suicide. After Six is released from the hospital, he notices a woman acting strangely at his friend's burial procession. Six talks with the woman, who tells him she was the friend's lover and that they were planning to escape from the island. She has a watch with a special device that will enable Six to evade Rover and steal a helicopter. Six takes the watch and "escapes" via the helicopter, but shortly after he has left the island he discovers the helicopter is rigged and controlled by Number Two. The episode ends with the helicopter returning to the Village and the spy friend, who had supposedly committed suicide, telling Number Two that Six is an unusual person who will need special treatment.

Although *The Prisoner* is not a fairy tale per se, it contains many of the same elements as a fairy tale. Many contemporary narrative texts are, it can be argued, modified and updated fairy tales that, to a considerable degree, resemble the tales Propp has described. Table 1.5 lists a few of the Proppian functions that can be applied to events in "Arrival." This analysis could be extended and made more detailed through the use of some of Propp's subcategories, but I only want to suggest the possibilities of this kind of analysis here.

There are two important things to be learned from syntagmatic analysis. First, narratives, regardless of kind or genre, are composed of certain functions (or elements) that are essential for the creation of a

TABLE 1.5 Proppian Functions in "Arrival" Episode of *The Prisoner*

Propp's Functions	Symbol	Events
Initial situation	a	Hero shown resigning
Interdiction violated	δ	(implicit) Spies can't resign
Villain causes injury	A	Hero abducted to the Village
Receipt of a magical agent	F	Woman gives Six watch with device
False hero exposed	Ex	Friend shown with Two

story. Propp's work leads us, then, to an understanding of the nature of formulas. Second, the order in which events take place in a narrative is of great importance. There is a logic to narrative texts, and the arrangement of elements in a story can greatly affect our perception of what anything "means." That, in fact, is the purpose served by editing.[1]

PARADIGMATIC ANALYSIS

The paradigmatic analysis of a text involves a search for a hidden pattern of oppositions that are buried in it and that generate meaning. As Alan Dundes writes in his introduction to Propp's *Morphology of the Folktale* (1928/1968), the paradigmatic form of structural analysis

> seeks to describe the pattern (usually based upon an a priori binary principle of opposition) which allegedly underlies the folkloristic text. This pattern is not the same as the sequential structure at all. Rather, the elements are taken out of the "given" order and are regrouped in one or more analytic schema. (p. xi)

We search for binary or polar oppositions because meaning is based on the establishment of relationships, and the most important kind of relationship in the production of meaning in language is that of opposition.

We return here to Saussure's (1966) notion that "in language there are only differences." Or, as Jonathan Culler (1976) has put it, "Structuralists have generally followed Jakobson and taken the binary opposition as a fundamental operation of the human mind basic to the production of meaning" (p. 15). Thus in all texts (whether narrative or not) there must be some kind of systematic and interrelated set of oppositions that can be elicited. Many people are not conscious of these oppositions—and sometimes they are only implied—but without differences, there is no meaning.

Some people argue that the oppositions and other structures that semioticians "elicit" from texts are not really there. These critics assert that semioticians do not *discover* systems of relationships but, instead, *invent* them. This controversy is sometimes known as the "hocus-pocus" versus the "God's truth" problem. I believe that the oppositions that semioticians find in texts are actually there; not only that, but they *have* to be there. Finding meaning without discerning polar oppositions is like listening to the sound of one hand clapping.

Given that I've used *The Prisoner* in an example above, let me offer a paradigmatic analysis of "Arrival." The most important opposition found in this episode is between freedom and control, and I use these two concepts at the head of my list of oppositions (Table 1.6). This brief listing shows the ideational structure upon which the narrative is hung.

Claude Lévi-Strauss, a distinguished French anthropologist, has suggested that a syntagmatic analysis of a text reveals the text's manifest meaning and that a paradigmatic analysis reveals the text's latent meaning. The manifest structure of a text consists of what happens in it, whereas the latent structure consists of what the text is about. Or, to put it another way, when we use a paradigmatic approach, we are not so much concerned with what characters *do* as with what they *mean.*

What Lévi-Strauss is interested in is the way narratives are organized or structured, and how their organization generates meaning. He has done a great deal of work (much of it highly controversial) on myths, kinship systems, and related matters. According to Lévi-Strauss (1967), myths are composed of fundamental or minimal units, "mythemes," that combine in certain ways to give messages. Mythemes can be expressed in short sentences that describe important relationships. For example, in the case of the Oedipus myth, Lévi-Strauss offers mythemes such as "Oedipus kills his father, Laius," "Oedipus marries his mother," and "Oedipus immolates the Sphinx." These mythemes and their rules of combination (what Lévi-Strauss calls "bundles," or relations) are the stuff of which myths are made. Myths are important not only because they function as charters for the groups that tell and believe them, but

TABLE 1.6 Polar Oppositions in "Arrival"

Freedom	*Control*
Number Six	Number Two
the individual	the organization
willpower	force
escape	entrapment
trust	deception

also because they are the keys to the ways in which the human mind works.

What is most significant about myths is the stories they tell, not their style. Thus the structured relationships among the characters and what these relationships ultimately mean should be the focus, not the way a story is told. Myths, Lévi-Strauss asserts, give coded messages from cultures to individuals, and the task of the analyst is to discover these masked or hidden messages by "cracking the code." In the final analysis, this involves eliciting the paradigmatic structure of a text.[2]

In making a paradigmatic analysis of a text, an analyst should take care to avoid certain possible errors. First, the analyst must be sure to elicit true oppositions (as opposed to mere negations). For example, I would suggest that "poor" is the opposite of "rich" and should be used instead of something such as "unrich" or "nonrich." Second, the analyst should be sure that the oppositions elicited are tied to characters and events in the text.

If I had offered a more detailed synopsis of "Arrival," I would have been able to undertake more detailed syntagmatic and paradigmatic analyses of this story, and my lists of Proppian functions and polar oppositions (Tables 1.5 and 1.6) would have been longer. I might add that it is useful for the analyst to explicate the terms used in his or her list of oppositions and to explain why each paired opposition is used.

INTERTEXTUALITY

Intertextuality is a term about which there is a good deal of controversy. For our purposes it will refer to the use in texts (consciously or unconsciously) of material from other, previously created texts. Parody, or the humorous imitation of a text, is a good example of the conscious reuse of material from a text. In order for parody to be effective, audience members must be familiar with the original text, so that they can appreciate the ways in which it is being ridiculed. There are also parodies of *style* (e.g., contests are held in which entrants compete to produce the most ridiculous imitation of Hemingway's writing style) and *genre* parodies, which play upon the basic plot structures of formulaic kinds of texts, such as soap operas and westerns.

Another kind of conscious intertextuality takes place when screenwriters or film directors create scenes that are recognizable as "quotations" from other films. Avant-garde filmmakers and other artists often consciously "quote" from the works of other artists—they patch together bits and pieces from well-known (or not so well-known) works and create new works.

Unconscious intertextuality involves textual materials of many kinds (plots, themes, kinds of characters, and so on) that become common currency, that pervade cultures, and that find their way into new texts without the creators' being aware of it. Some literary theorists argue, in fact, that all creative work is, ultimately, intertextual. That is, all texts are related to other texts, to varying degrees.

The Russian semiotician Mikhail Bakhtin has suggested that language is "dialogic," by which he means that when we speak, what we say is tied both to things that have been said before and to utterances that we expect to be made in the future. If we take this notion and move it from speech utterances to texts, we can gain some insight into intertexuality. In a book of essays titled *The Dialogic Imagination* (1981), Bakhtin discusses the relationships that exist among texts. Bakhtin writes about what he calls the matter of "quotation" (which we now call intertextuality) in the Middle Ages:

> The role of the other's word was enormous at that time; there were quotations that were openly and reverently emphasized as such, or that were half-hidden, completely hidden, half-conscious, unconscious, correct, intentionally distorted, deliberately reinterpreted and so forth. The boundary lines between someone else's speech and one's own speech were flexible, ambiguous, often deliberately distorted and confused. Certain types of texts were constructed like mosaics out of the texts of others. . . . One of the best authorities on medieval par-

ody . . . states outright that the history of medieval literature and its
Latin literature in particular "is the history of appropriation, re-work-
ing and imitation of someone else's property"—or as we would say,
of another's language, another's style, another's word. (p. 69)

The "appropriation" of the work of others that took place in the Middle
Ages is similar to what happens today. This is because, in part, many
inhabitants of the Western world share a common cultural heritage that
informs the work of artists and is reflected in texts even when there is
no conscious decision made to "quote" from other texts or sources.

METAPHOR AND METONYMY

Metaphor and metonymy are two important ways of transmitting
meaning. In metaphor, a relationship between two things is suggested
through the use of *analogy*. Thus we might say, "My love is a red rose."
One of the most common metaphoric forms is the simile, in which *like*
or *as* is used and a comparison is suggested. For example, "He's as sharp
as a razor" or "She's as good as an angel."

Sometimes we incorporate metaphors and similes into the verbs we
use. Consider the following examples:

The ship *cut* through the waves. (The ship is like a knife.)
The ship *danced* through the waves. (The ship is like a dancer.)
The ship *raced* through the waves. (The ship is like a race car.)
The ship *pranced* through the waves. (The ship is like a horse.)
The ship *plowed* through the waves. (The ship is like a plow.)

In these examples, the ship takes on different identities. These verbs
convey information that is different from that in the statement "The ship
sailed through the waves."

In metonymy, a relationship is suggested that is based on *association*,
which implies the existence of codes in people's minds that enable them
to make the proper connections. As James Monaco (1977) has noted:

A metonymy is a figure of speech in which an associated detail or
notion is used to invoke an idea or represent an object. Etymologically,

the word means "substitute naming" (from the Greek meta, involving transfer, and onoma, name). Thus in literature we can speak of the king (and the idea of kingship) as "the crown." (p. 135)

A common form of metonymy is a synecdoche, in which a part stands for the whole or vice versa.

A good example of metaphor in film is the famous scene in Chaplin's *The Gold Rush* in which he cooks his boots and eats the shoelaces as if they were spaghetti. A good example of metonymy is found in *The Prisoner* in the form of the monstrous balloon Rover, which symbolizes the oppressive regime that runs the Village. Table 1.7 compares and contrasts metaphor and metonymy.

Generally speaking, metaphor and metonymy are often mixed together, and sometimes a given object might have both metaphoric and metonymic significance. The distinction is important, because it enables us to see more clearly how objects and images (as well as language) generate meaning. And, in the case of metonymy, it becomes obvious that people carry *codes* around in their heads—highly complex patterns of associations that enable them to interpret metonymic communication correctly. Just as you can't tell the players without a program, you can't understand the meaning of most things without knowing the codes.

CODES

Codes are highly complex patterns of associations that all members of a given society and culture learn. These codes, or "secret structures" in people's minds, affect the ways that individuals interpret the signs and symbols they find in the media and the ways they live. From this perspective, cultures are codification systems that play an important (though often unperceived) role in people's lives. To be socialized and to be a member of a culture means, in essence, to be taught a number of codes, most of which are quite specific to a person's social class, geographic location, ethnic group, and so on, though these subcodings may exist within a more general code, such as "American character," for example.

We all recognize that in order for people to be able to drive safely on the highways, a code is needed. This code is a collection of rules that tells drivers what they should and should not do in all conceivable

TABLE 1.7 Metaphor and Metonymy Contrasted

Metaphor	*Metonymy*
Meta (transfer, beyond)-*phor* (to bear)	*Meta* (transfer)-*onoma* (name)
Chaplin eats shoelaces like spaghetti.	Rover kills one of the villagers on command of Number Two.
Simile: important subcategory in which comparison is made using *like* or *as*.	*Synecdoche:* important subcategory in which part stands for the whole or whole for a part.
"No man is an island . . . "	Red suggests passion.
Costume of Spider-Man.	Uncle Sam "stands" for United States.
Long, thin objects can be seen as penises.	Bowler hat implies Englishman; cowboy hat implies the American West.

situations. In like manner, we are all taught (often informally) other codes that tell us what to do in various situations and what certain things "mean." Obviously, we carry these rules and understandings about life over to our exposure to media productions, or to *mass-mediated culture.*

It is quite possible, then, for misunderstandings to arise between those who create television programs and those who view them. Umberto Eco (1972) has even suggested that "aberrant decoding . . . is the rule in the mass media" (p. 106). This is because different people bring different codes to given messages and thus interpret the messages in different ways. As Eco puts it:

> Codes and subcodes are applied to the message [read "text"] in the light of a general framework of cultural references, which constitutes the receiver's patrimony of knowledge: his ideological, ethical, religious standpoints, his psychological attitudes, his tastes, his value systems, etc. (p. 115)

Eco offers some examples that suggest how such aberrant decodings might have taken place in the past: foreigners in strange cultures who do not know the codes, or people who interpret messages in terms of their own codes rather than the codes in which the messages were originally cast. This was, Eco notes, before the development of mass media, when aberrant decodings were the exception, not the rule. With the development of mass media, however, the situation changed radically, and aberrant decoding became the norm. According to Eco, this is because of the wide gap that exists between those who create and generate the material carried by the media and those who receive this material.

The transmitters of messages, because of their social class, educational level, political ideologies, worldviews, ethos, and so on, do not share the same codes as their audiences, who differ from the message transmitters in some or even most of the above respects and who interpret the messages they receive from their own perspectives. The work of British sociolinguist Basil Bernstein (1977) illustrates how this might be possible. His research led him to conclude that in Britain, children learn either of two linguistic codes, the "elaborated" code or the "restrictive" code, and that the code a child learns plays a major role in his or her future development and adult life. The following lists show the differences between these two codes:

Elaborated Code	Restricted Code
middle classes	working classes
grammatically complex	grammatically simple
varied vocabulary	uniform vocabulary
complex sentence structure	short, repetitious sentences
careful use of adjectives and adverbs	little use of adjectives and adverbs
high-level conceptualization	low-level conceptualization
logical	emotional
use of qualifications	little use of qualifications
users aware of code	users unaware of code

The code a child learns becomes the matrix through which his or her thought is filtered; thus the two codes lead to very different value systems, belief systems, attitudes about the world, and so on. Bernstein's work enables us to see how language shapes us and demonstrates the enormous problems we face in trying to resocialize the hard-core poor and other disadvantaged elements in society.

It has been said that the United States and Great Britain are two nations separated by a common language. In the same manner, the different classes in Britain, with their different codes, seem to be separated. When we move from language to the mass media, where in addition there are aesthetic codes, iconic codes, and more separating audience members, we can see that it is quite remarkable that the media can communicate with any degree of effectiveness.

Although I cannot address them in any detail here, there are several further aspects of codes and questions related to them that I would like to mention briefly; readers who are interested in investigating the subject of codes would do well to consider the following list:

- ✔ *Characteristics of codes:* coherence, covertness, clarity, concreteness, continuity, comprehensiveness, and so on
- ✔ *Manifestations of codes:* personality (in psychology), social roles (in social psychology), institutions (in sociology), ideologies (in political science), rituals (in anthropology)
- ✔ *Problems:* creation of codes, modification of codes, conflicting codes, countercodes, codes and rules
- ✔ *Codes in popular culture:* formulas in spy stories, detective stories, westerns, science fiction adventures, pop music, fanzines, girlie fiction, horror stories, gothic novels, advertisements, sitcoms, and so on
- ✔ *Ritual:* mealtimes, drinking in bars, gift giving, dating, television watching, supermarket shopping, behavior in elevators, sports contests, lovemaking, dressing, and so on[3]

Codes are difficult to see because of their characteristics—they are all-pervasive, specific, and clear-cut, which makes them almost invisible. They inform almost every aspect of our existence (I've listed some of their manifestations) and provide a useful concept for the analyst of the popular arts and media; for not only do genres such as the western and the sitcom follow codes (commonly known as formulas), so do the media in general. It is to this subject I would like to turn now, specifically, with a discussion of codes in television.

SEMIOTICS OF THE TELEVISION MEDIUM

I have, to this point, been concerned with the ways semiotic analysis can be used to explicate programs carried on television, with a specific focus on the television narrative. Various forms of media carry various genres of the popular arts, as the following lists demonstrate:

Media	*Popular Art Forms*
radio	soap operas
television	advertisements/commercials
films	westerns
comics	police dramas
records	variety shows
posters	musicals
newspapers	talk shows
magazines	news
telephone	spy stories
books	documentaries
billboards	love stories

Each medium, because of its nature, imposes certain limitations on whatever popular art forms or genres it carries. Because of the small screen and the nature of the television image, for instance, television is not the ideal medium for presenting huge battle scenes. Television is a "close-up" medium, better suited to revealing character than to capturing action.

In applying semiotics to television, then, it makes sense for us to concern ourselves with aspects of the medium that *function as* signs, as distinguished from *carrying* signs. What is interesting about television, from this point of view, are the kinds of camera shots employed in the medium. Here is a list of some of the most important kinds of shots, which function as signifiers, and what is usually signified by each shot.

Signifier (shot)	*Definition*	*Signified (meaning)*
close-up	face only	intimacy
medium shot	most of body	personal relationship
long shot	setting and characters	context, scope, public distance
full shot	full body of person	social relationship

Camera work and editing techniques can be examined in the same way.

Signifier	*Definition*	*Signified*
pan down	camera looks down	power, authority
pan up	camera looks up	smallness, weakness
dolly in	camera moves in	observation, focus
fade in	image appears on blank screen	beginning
fade out	image screen goes blank	ending
cut	switch from one image to another	simultaneity, excitement
wipe	image wiped off screen	imposed conclusion

The above material represents a kind of grammar of television as far as shots, camera work, and editing techniques are concerned. We all learn the meanings of these phenomena as we watch television, and they help us to understand what is going on in particular programs.

There are other matters that might be considered here also, such as lighting techniques, the use of color, sound effects, and music. All of these are signifiers that help us to interpret what we see (and also what we hear) on television. Television is a highly complex medium that uses verbal language, visual images, and sound to generate impressions and ideas in people. It is the task of the television semiotician to determine, first, how this is possible and, second, how this is accomplished.

SOME CRITICISMS OF SEMIOTIC ANALYSIS

You will notice that I have said very little up to this point about aesthetic judgments. This leads us to one of the major criticisms of semiotic analysis, namely, that in its concern for the relationship of elements and production of meaning in a text, it ignores the quality of the work itself. That is, semiotics is not really concerned with art, but rather with meaning and modes of cognition (the codes needed to understand a text). It may be compared to judging a meal by the quality of the ingredients, without any concern for how the food was cooked or what it tasted like.

In certain cases, the text is subjugated by the critic. It exists as nothing but (or perhaps little more than) an excuse for a virtuoso performance by the semiotician, who grabs the spotlight away from the work itself. But this is a problem of all forms of interpretation. Most works of art exist now at the top of a huge mountain of criticism that analyzes and explicates them, sometimes at greater length than the original works themselves.

Another problem with semiotic analysis, especially of television and televised texts, is that a strong theoretical foundation is lacking that would facilitate work in this area. Most of the work done in semiotics in recent years has been concerned with film, not television. Without a strong and well-articulated body of theoretical criticism, work in the applied semiotic analysis of television texts must remain tentative.

Nevertheless, a great deal is possible, and if you can avoid extremism in your analyses of signifying systems in texts, you can produce critical readings of considerable value and utility. You have enough theory to get started, and applied semiotic analyses are likely to lead to advances in critical theory.

A CHECKLIST FOR SEMIOTIC
ANALYSIS OF TELEVISION

I suggest below some of the questions you should address in undertaking a semiotic analysis of a television program. I have concentrated on narratives in this chapter, but much of what I have discussed is applicable to all kinds of programs.

Isolate and analyze the important signs in your text.
> What are the important signifiers and what do they signify?
> What is the system that gives these signs meaning?
> What codes can be found?
> What ideological and sociological matters are involved?

What is the paradigmatic structure of the text?
> What is the central opposition in the text?
> What paired opposites fit under the various categories?
> Do these oppositions have any psychological or social import?

What is the syntagmatic structure of the text?
> Which of Propp's functions can be applied to the text?
> How does the sequential arrangement of elements affect meaning?
> Are there formulaic aspects that have shaped the text?

How does the medium of television affect the text?
> What kinds of shots, camera angles, and editing techniques are used?
> How are lighting, color, music, and sound used to give meaning to signs?

What contributions have theorists made that can be applied?
> What have theorists in semiotics written that can be adapted to your analysis of television?
> What have media theorists written that can be applied to semiotic analysis?

I hope that the contents of this chapter have given you a sense of the semiotic approach and will enable you to apply this fascinating—and powerful—analytic tool. You can apply semiotics to television, film, the comics, advertisements, architecture, medical diseases, artifacts, objects, formulas, conventions, organizations, friends, enemies, and just about anything else in which communication is important—and in which there is signification.

STUDY QUESTIONS AND TOPICS FOR DISCUSSION

1. Contrast the work of Peirce and Saussure on the nature of signs.
2. Discuss the following concepts: synchronic/diachronic, syntagmatic/paradigmatic, language/speaking, metaphor/metonymy, elaborated/restricted codes.
3. Explain, in detail, Propp's theory. Discuss his ideas about "functions" in narrative texts.
4. What significance does binary opposition have? What does it mean to say that concepts are "purely differential"?
5. What are codes? Why are they important?
6. Discuss the assertions in this chapter concerning how camera shots in television and film function as signs.
7. What are the differences between elaborated and restricted codes?
8. What criticisms can be made of semiotic analysis?

ANNOTATED BIBLIOGRAPHY

Bakhtin, M. M. (1981). *The dialogic imagination: Four essays* (Michael Holquist, Ed.; Caryl Emerson and Michael Holquist, Trans.). Austin: University of Texas Press. This volume consists of four essays on literary theory, with a focus on the novel. After years of obscurity, Bakhtin has been "discovered," and his ideas have become extremely influential, especially his notion of dialogism, discussed in this book, and of "carnival," discussed in his book on Rabelais.

Barthes, Roland. (1970). *Writing degree zero and elements of semiology* (A. Lavers & C. Smith, Trans.). Boston: Beacon. Barthes addresses the basic concepts used in semiotic analysis and makes reference to some of the work he has done on food, fashion, furniture, and automobiles.

Barthes, Roland. (1972). *Mythologies.* New York: Hill & Wang. This volume is a collection of short essays on everyday-life topics, such as wrestling, soap powders, margarine, and steak and chips, and a long essay on semiotic aspects of myth. This is a fascinating book and one of the most interesting examples of applied semiotic analysis available.

Berger, Arthur Asa. (1997). *Bloom's morning: Coffee, comforters, and the hidden meaning of everyday life.* Boulder, CO: Westview. This book takes an everyman named Bloom (after the hero of Joyce's *Ulysses*) and analyzes the semiotic significance of every object he uses and everything he does from the moment he is awakened by his radio alarm clock to the time he has breakfast. The 35 short essays on Bloom's morning are preceded by a discussion of everyday life, and the book ends with a chapter titled "Myth, Culture, and Everyday Life"; the book is illustrated with more than 35 drawings by the author.

Berger, Arthur Asa. (1997). *Seeing is believing: An introduction to visual communication* (2nd ed.). Mountain View, CA: Mayfield. This book functions as a primer to help readers become visually literate. Subjects covered include basic elements of visual communication; photography, film, television, comics, and cartoons; typography; and new technologies related to visual communication.

Berger, Arthur Asa. (1998). *Signs in contemporary culture: An introduction to semiotics* (2nd ed.). Salem, WI: Sheffield. This book is intended for people who have no familiarity with semiotic thought. It offers an exploration of the basic concepts of semiotic theory, along with applications of these concepts to various aspects of contemporary society. Each chapter contains both discussion and application of a semiotic concept.

Coward, Rosalind, & Ellis, John. (1977). *Language and materialism: Developments in semiology and the theory of the subject.* London: Routledge & Kegan Paul. This is an important theoretical work that deals with semiotics and its relation to Marxism, the work of French post-Freudian Lacan, and other topics.

Culler, Jonathan. (1976). *Structuralist poetics: Structuralism, linguistics and the study of literature.* Ithaca, NY: Cornell University Press. Culler provides an excellent discussion of the basic principles of semiotic analysis and application to literature. Another book by Culler, *Ferdinand de Saussure* (in the Penguin Modern Masters series) is also highly recommended.

Eco, Umberto. (1976). *A theory of semiotics.* Bloomington: Indiana University Press. This book contains an important theoretical analysis of semiotics that deals with its range of applications; it is an advanced text for readers with a good background in the subject. See also Eco's *The Role of the Reader: Explorations in the Semiotics of Texts* (Indiana University Press, 1979).

Fiske, John, & Hartley, John. (1978). *Reading television.* London: Methuen. This is one of the most useful applications of semiotic theory to television to be found. The authors devote a good deal of attention to codes and to specific texts.

Goldman, Robert, & Papson, Stephen. (1996). *Sign wars: The cluttered landscape of advertising.* New York: Guilford. Using semiotics and other methods of cultural criticism, the authors "decode" advertising in general and various commercials and ad campaigns in particular. They also discuss, from a critical perspective, advertising's role in U.S. culture and society.

Gottdiener, Mark. (1995). *Postmodern semiotics: Material culture and the forms of postmodern life.* Oxford: Basil Blackwell. Gottdiener is a sociologist who uses semiotic analysis (among other things) to analyze shopping malls, Disneyland, and postmodern architecture. The first part of the book is devoted to theoretical concerns (and is complicated and very sophisticated); the second part addresses cultural studies and sociosemiotics.

Guiraud, Pierre. (1975). *Semiology.* London: Routledge & Kegan Paul. This is a very brief but interesting explication of semiotic principles, originally published in the French "Que sais-je?" series. It focuses on the functions of media, signification, and codes.

Leach, Edmund. (1970). *Claude Lévi-Strauss.* New York: Viking. This book represents one of the more successful attempts to make Lévi-Strauss understandable to the general reader. It includes some biographical material as well as chapters on myth, kinship, and symbolism.

Lévi-Strauss, Claude. (1967). *Structural anthropology*. Garden City, NY: Doubleday. This volume is a collection of essays on language, kinship, social organization, magic, religion, and art by the distinguished French anthropologist, an original mind and a great literary stylist.

Lotman, Jurij (Yuri) M. (1976). *Semiotics of cinema* (Mark E. Suino, Trans.). Ann Arbor: Michigan Slavic Contributions. This book is an application of semiotics to cinema that deals with narration, montage, plot, acting, and other related topics. Lotman is identified with the Tartu school of Russian semiotics and applies its principles to art and culture. Another of Lotman's books, *The Structure of the Artistic Text*, has also been published by Michigan Slavic Contributions (located at the University of Michigan).

Propp, Vladimir. (1968). *Morphology of the folktale*. Austin: University of Texas Press. This is a classic "formalist" analysis of fairy tales, originally published in 1928, that has implications for the analysis of all kinds of other mass-mediated culture.

Saussure, Ferdinand de. (1966). *A course in general linguistics* (W. Baskin, Trans.). New York: McGraw-Hill. This is one of the central documents in semiotic analysis and the source of many of the concepts used in the field.

Scholes, Robert. (1974). *Structuralism in literature*. New Haven, CT: Yale University Press. This book provides an introduction to structuralism, with a focus on the analysis of literary texts but with obvious implications for other kinds of texts. The ideas of such thinkers as Jakobson, Lévi-Strauss, Jolles, Souriau, Propp, and Barthes are presented.

Sebeok, Thomas A. (Ed.). (1977). *A perfusion of signs.*/(1978). *Sight, sound and sense.* Bloomington: Indiana University Press. These two volumes edited by Sebeok are important collections of applied semiotic theory. The topics addressed include clowns, medicine, faces, religion, nonsense, architecture, music, and culture.

Solomon, Jack. (1988). *The signs of our times: The secret meanings of everyday life*. New York: Harper & Row. This book presents a fascinating and perceptive application of semiotic analysis to everything from advertising, toys, and architecture to television, food, and fashion. It has an excellent concluding chapter on postmodernist art forms such as MTV and postmodernist works such as the film *Koyaanisqatsi*.

Wright, Will. (1975). *Sixguns and society: A structural study of the western*. Berkeley: University of California Press. This is an ingenious application of the ideas of Lévi-Strauss, Propp, and others to the western.

NOTES

1. For example, consider the difference order makes in the following two phrases, both of which contain the same words: "My husband was late . . . " and "My late husband was . . . ."

2. Space does not permit me to dwell any longer on Lévi-Strauss. Readers interested in pursuing this subject are referred to the annotated bibliography that accompanies this chapter for works by and about this author.

3. For an explication of these matters, see Berger (1976a).

Marxist thought is one of the most powerful and suggestive ways available to the media analyst for analyzing society and its institutions. This chapter deals with such fundamental principles of Marxist analysis as alienation, materialism, false consciousness, class conflict, and hegemony—concepts that can be applied to media and can help us understand the ways media function. Particular attention is paid to the role of advertising in creating consumer lust, and some cautions are offered about the danger of being doctrinaire.

CHAPTER 2

Marxist Analysis

U ntil a decade or so ago, there was rather little Marxist analysis in
"mainstream" American literary and social thought. This is not to
say that there were no Marxists; rather, the Marxists were always
"voices crying in the wilderness"—not very many people took heed of
these voices or took them seriously. This has been changing in recent
years, and there are now increasing numbers of Marxist historians,
political scientists, economists, and critics.

The situation is complicated by the fact that there are a variety of
kinds, or schools, of Marxism, and Marxist thought seems to be changing rapidly. In the pages that follow I will offer a discussion of some of
the more fundamental concepts of Marxism that can be applied to
media and popular culture. Ironically, Marxism today often seems to
have more interesting things to say about culture, consciousness, and
related problems than it does about economics.

The discussion that follows leans heavily on the work of Erich
Fromm, who has argued that Marx was a humanist whose argument
was essentially a moral one. I might point out, in passing, that many
Marxists do not approve of the societies, created in his name but
perverting his doctrine, found in the former Soviet Union, Eastern
Europe, Cuba, China, and elsewhere. That is, one can be a Marxist
without being a communist, and without believing in the necessity of
revolution and establishment of a classless society by violent means.

What follows is an outline of some of the most fundamental principles of Marxism—principles that will be most useful for the media

analyst. My plan is to provide a basic understanding of Marxism, so that readers can apply Marxist concepts to the public art forms carried by the media. Readers who find that this kind of analysis offers them valuable new perspectives and leads to new insights can pursue study of the subject further (see, for instance, the books listed in the annotated bibliography that accompanies this chapter). I will cite a number of texts that will be helpful, but, because of the limitations of space, this chapter can form no more than an introduction to Marxist thought that can be used to make applied Marxist analyses of media.

MATERIALISM

When we talk about Marxist thought being *materialistic,* we are using the term in a special way—not as it is traditionally used in the United States, where it suggests a craving for money and the things that money can buy. For Marxists, materialism is more of a conception of history and the way society organizes itself. Let me start here with some quotations of crucial importance from Marx's *Preface to a Contribution to the Critique of Political Economy* (1964). First, his discussion of the relationship that exists between society and consciousness:

> In the social production which men carry on they enter into definite relations that are indispensable and independent of their will; these relations of production correspond to a definite state of development of their material powers of production. The totality of these relations of production constitutes the economic structure of society—the real foundation, on which legal and political superstructures arise and to which definite forms of social consciousness correspond. The mode of production of material life determines the general character of the social, political and spiritual processes of life. It is not the consciousness of men that determines their being, but, on the contrary, their social being determines their consciousness. (p. 51)

The mode of production—economic relationships—then, is the base or the "determinant element" in our thoughts—though the relationship between our thoughts and society is a complicated one. This passage suggests that beneath the superficial randomness of things there is a kind of inner logic at work. Everything is shaped, ultimately, by the economic system of a society, which, in subtle ways, affects the ideas that individuals have, ideas that are instrumental in determining the kinds of arrangements people will make with one another, the institutions they will establish, and so on.

Marx also wrote, in *The German Ideology* (1964):

> The production of ideas, of conceptions, of consciousness, is at first directly interwoven with the material activity and the material intercourse of men, the language of real life. Conceiving, thinking, the mental intercourse of men, appear at this stage as the direct efflux from their material behavior. The same applies to mental production as expressed in the language of politics, laws, morality, religion, metaphysics of a people. Men are the producers of their conceptions, ideas, etc.—real, active men, as they are conditioned by the definite development of their productive forces and of the intercourse corresponding to these, up to its furthest forms. Consciousness can never be anything else than conscious existence. (pp. 74-75)

This passage is important because it brings people into the picture and suggests that though consciousness is socially produced, it is always filtered through the minds of real, live, active men and women and is not something that works automatically. There is always the possibility of individuals' gaining an understanding of their situation and doing something about it. But more about this shortly. We have, now, our first important insight—namely, that "our" ideas are not entirely our own, that knowledge is social.

With all of the above in mind, there are some questions we might ask now:

1. What social, political, and economic arrangements characterize the society in which the media are being analyzed?
2. Who owns, controls, and operates the media?
3. What roles do the various media play in the society where the media are being analyzed? And what are the functions of the various popular art forms carried by the media?
4. What ideas, values, notions, concepts, beliefs, and so on are spread by the media, and what ideas, values, and so on are neglected by the media? Why?
5. How are writers, artists, actors, and other creative people affected by the patterns of ownership and control of the media?

THE BASE AND THE SUPERSTRUCTURE

In this section I begin to develop ideas found in the passages quoted earlier. What Marx has described as the "base" represents the economic system found in a given society. This economic system, or mode of production, influences, in profound and complicated ways, the "superstructure," or institutions and values, of a given society. Here is a relevant quotation from Friedrich Engels's "Socialism: Utopian and Scientific" (1972) on this matter:

> The new facts made imperative a new examination of all past history. Then it was seen that *all* past history, with the exception of its primitive stages, was the history of class struggles; that these warring classes of society are always the products of the modes of production and of exchange—in a word, of the *economic* conditions of their time; that the economic structure of society always furnishes the real basis, starting from which we can alone work out the ultimate explanation of the whole superstructure of juridical and political institutions as well as of the religious, philosophical, and other ideas of a given historical period. Hegel had freed history from metaphysics—he had made it dialectical; but his conception of history was essentially idealistic. But now idealism was driven from its last refuge, the philosophy of history; now a materialistic treatment of history was propounded, and a method found of explaining man's "knowing" by his "being" instead of, as heretofore, his "being" by his "knowing." (p. 621)

What this passage offers is an explanation of how ideas are transmitted to human beings—through the institutions, philosophical systems, religious organizations, and arts found in a given society at a given time—that is, through the superstructure. Capitalism is not only an economic system but also something that affects attitudes, values, personality types, and culture in general.

How the base affects the superstructure is a problem that has caused a considerable amount of aggravation to Marxists. Economic relations may be the ultimately determining ones, but they are not the only ones, and it is a great oversimplification to say that the superstructure is automatically shaped by the base and is nothing but a reflection of it—a position sometimes described as "vulgar Marxism." This point of view fails to recognize that an economic system is dynamic and always in a state of change—as is a given superstructure—and that people, leading real lives and capable of all kinds of actions, are involved also. In the following discussion of superstructure I will focus on the public arts and the mass media, institutions that many Marxists claim are crucial to the understanding of how consciousness is determined, shaped, and manipulated.

Figure 2.1 displays the ideas I've just discussed in diagrammatic form. All of this might seem rather abstract and irrelevant until one recognizes that the consciousness of people has important social, economic, and political implications.

FALSE CONSCIOUSNESS AND IDEOLOGY

It is important for the ruling class to affect people's consciousness by giving them certain ideas; in this way the wealthy, who benefit most from the social arrangements in a capitalist country, maintain the status quo. Marx (1964) explains how the ruling class operates:

> The ideas of the ruling class are, in every age, the ruling ideas: i.e., the class which is the dominant *material* force in society is at the same time its dominant *intellectual* force. The class which has the means of material production at its disposal, has control at the same time over the means of mental production, so that in consequence the ideas of those who lack the means of mental production are, in general, subject to it. The dominant ideas are nothing more than the ideal expression of the dominant material relationships, the dominant material relationships grasped as ideas, and thus of the relationships which make one class the ruling one; they are consequently the ideas of its dominance. The individuals composing the ruling class possess among other things consciousness, and therefore think. Insofar, therefore, as they rule as a class and determine the whole extent of an epoch, it is self-evident that they do this in their whole range and thus, among other things, rule also as thinkers, as producers of ideas, and regulate the production and distribution of the ideas of their age. Consequently their ideas are the ruling ideas of their age. (p. 78)

According to this thesis, the ideas of a given age are those promulgated and popularized by the ruling class in its own interest. Generally speaking, then, the ideas people have are the ideas that the ruling class wants them to have.

Base   Mode of Production
                                        (system of economic relations)

↓   ↓

Superstructure   Institutions
                                              legal system
                                              philosophy
                                              religion
                                              ideas
                                              arts
                                              culture

Figure 2.1. Influences on the Superstructure

The ruling class, we must recognize, believes its own messages. This is because it has within itself a group of conceptualizing ideologists who, as Marx puts it, "make it their chief source of livelihood to develop and perfect the illusions of the class about itself" (p. 79). By *ideology*, I mean any system of logically coherent and widely applicable socio-political beliefs. The ruling class, according to this theory, propagates an ideology that justifies its status and makes it difficult for ordinary people to recognize that they are being exploited and victimized.

This notion—that the masses of people are being manipulated and exploited by the ruling class—is one of the central arguments of modern Marxist cultural analysis. As Donald Lazere (1977) notes:

> Applied to any aspect of culture, Marxist method seeks to explicate the manifest and latent or coded reflections of modes of material production, ideological values, class relations and structures of social power—racial or sexual as well as politico-economic—or the state of consciousness of people in a precise historical or socio-economic situation. . . . The Marxist method, recently in varying degrees of combination with structuralism and semiology, has provided an incisive analytic tool for studying the political signification in every facet of contemporary culture, including popular entertainment in TV and films, music, mass circulation books, newspaper and magazine features, comics, fashion, tourism, sports and games, as well as such acculturating institutions as education, religion, the family and child-rearing, social and sexual relations between men and women—all the

patterns of work, play, and other customs of everyday life. . . . The most frequent theme in Marxist cultural criticism is the way the prevalent mode of production and the ideology of the ruling class in any society dominate every phase of culture, and at present, the way capitalist production and ideology dominate American culture, along with that of the rest of the world that American business and culture have colonized. This domination is perpetuated both through overt propaganda in political rhetoric, news reporting, advertising and public relations, and through the often unconscious absorption of capitalistic values by creators and consumers in all the above aspects of the culture of everyday life. (pp. 755-756)

This passage suggests the all-encompassing nature of the Marxist approach and some of the most important objects of its attention. Quite obviously, the mass media and popular culture are centrally important in the spread of false consciousness, in leading people to believe that "whatever is, is right." From this perspective the mass media and popular culture constitute a crucial link between the institutions of society (and the superstructure in general) and individual consciousness.

The notion of manipulation has been attacked by German media theorist Hans Magnus Enzenberger (1974) as being useful but perhaps a bit dated:

The New Left of the sixties has reduced the development of the media to a single concept—that of manipulation. This concept was originally extremely useful for heuristic purposes and has made possible a great many individual analytical investigations, but it now threatens to degenerate into a mere slogan which conceals more than it is able to illuminate, and therefore itself requires analysis. (pp. 100-101)

Enzenberger argues that the notion of manipulation is ultimately grounded on the assumption (the unspoken premise) that "there is such a thing as pure, unmanipulated truth," a notion he finds questionable, and one that is too limited. Ultimately, he argues, the left's antagonism toward mass media benefits capitalism.

Enzenberger's hope is, perhaps, somewhat utopian. His notion is that all media manipulate; it is in the very nature of media:

> There is no such thing as unmanipulated writing, filming, or broad-casting. The question is therefore not whether the media are manipu-lated, but who manipulates them. A revolutionary plan should not require the manipulators to disappear; on the contrary, it must make everyone a manipulator. (p. 104)

At this point we have moved away from analysis per se, and I will not pursue Enzenberger's thought any further. It may be that the theory of manipulation has deficiencies and drawbacks, but it still remains a central concept of Marxist media analysis for the simple reason that, as Marxists view society, the media are tools of manipulation. (The same argument about media manipulation can be used against socialist and communist countries, though Marxist critics as a rule do not like to concern themselves with such matters.)

CLASS CONFLICT

For Marx, history is based on unending class conflict—unending, that is, until the establishment of a communist society, in which classes disappear and, with them, conflict.

> The history of all hitherto existing society is the history of class struggles. Freeman and slave, patrician and plebeian, lord and serf, guild-master and journeyman, in a word oppressor and oppressed, stood in constant opposition to one another, carried on an uninter-rupted, now hidden, now open fight, a fight that each time ended either in a revolutionary reconstitution of society at large, or in the common ruin of the contending classes. (Marx, 1964, p. 200)

The two classes that Marx talks about are the bourgeoisie, who own the factories and corporations and form the ruling class, and the proletariat, the huge mass of workers who are exploited by this ruling class and whose condition becomes increasingly more desperate.

The bourgeoisie, according to this theory, avert class conflict by indoctrinating the proletariat with "ruling-class ideas," such as the notion of "the self-made man" and the idea that the social and economic arrangements in a given society are "natural" and not "historical." If social arrangements are natural, they cannot be modified; thus one must accept a given order as inevitable. Marxists argue that the social and economic arrangements found in a given society at a given time are historical—created by people and therefore capable of being changed by people. The bourgeoisie try to convince everyone that capitalism is natural and therefore eternal, but this idea, say the Marxists, is patently false, and it is the duty of Marxist analysts to demonstrate this.

One of the approaches the ruling class uses is to convince people that there are no classes in a given society or that class is somehow incidental and irrelevant. Thus in the United States we have the myth of a "classless" society because we have not had a hereditary aristocracy and because members of the upper class tend to be friendly in social encounters. The president of a major corporation might call the doorman or janitor by his first name, but this, to the Marxists, is a means of camouflaging the real social relations that exist—although the United States, with its large middle class, does present special problems to Marxist analysts, as the likelihood of a revolution seems rather distant.

Nevertheless, the mass media still perform their job of distracting people from the realities of U.S. society (poverty, racism, sexism, and so on) and of "clouding their minds" with ideas that the ruling class wishes them to have. In some cases, the media offer heroes who reflect the bourgeois, ruling-class line and who reinforce and indoctrinate the masses who follow their activities in books, television programs, films, and so on. Generally speaking, the media serve either to mask class differences or to act as apologists for the ruling class in an effort to avert class conflict and prevent changes in the political order.

But the fact remains that for Marxists, classes exist, and members of opposing classes are locked into hostile and mutually destructive relationships. As Marx (1964) has written, "Society as a whole is more and more splitting up into two great hostile camps, into two great classes directly facing each other—bourgeoisie and proletariat" (p. 201). The resolution of this dialectic is, for Marxists, inevitable, even though the media controlled by the ruling class or bourgeoisie may temporarily prevent members of the proletariat from attaining true consciousness of their situation.

Henri Lefebvre (1968/1984), a French Marxist, has taken the concept of class conflict and manipulation and developed it into the notion that people living in capitalist societies are living in a state of "terror." He explains this notion as follows. First, any society with radical class differences, with a small privileged class at the top and a mass of people living in poverty, has to be maintained through compulsion and persuasion. Second, such a class-stratified society is bound to become overly repressive and must develop sophisticated ways of masking repression and making unsuspecting individuals the instruments of their own repression and the repression of others. Finally, we arrive at the "terrorist" society, in which

> compulsion and the illusion of freedom converge; unacknowledged compulsions besiege the lives of communities (and of their individual members) and organize them according to a general strategy. . . . In a terrorist society terror is diffuse, violence is always latent, pressure is exerted from all sides on its members, who can only avoid it and shift its weight by a super-human effort; each member is a terrorist because he wants to be in power (if only briefly). . . . the "system" . . . has a hold on every member separately and submits every member to the whole, that is, to a strategy, a hidden end, objectives unknown to all but those in power, and that no one questions. (p. 147)

This notion, that people who live in capitalist societies are living in a state of terror, may seem extreme at first, but it may help to explain why many Americans feel pressured and anxious about their lives and their prospects for the future.

Lefebvre first wrote his book in 1968, when Marxism seemed to have answers for people and when the critiques it made of bourgeois societies seemed terribly telling. Marxists spoke from a sense of moral superiority when they criticized class-ridden capitalist societies, full of exploited workers and impoverished people.

The events in the 1990s in Eastern Europe and the Soviet Union have shown that the Marxist-Leninist governments in these states only pretended to rule in the people's interest. They were class-ridden and corrupt, and grossly inefficient as well. The rapid decline of communism as a viable form of government has cast a dark shadow on Lefebvre's criticisms of capitalist societies. In reality, it could be argued that it was the communist societies that were terrorist, both overtly (in their use of military power and the secret police) and in terms of their impact on the psyches of their citizens.

And yet it strikes me that Lefebvre's argument has some merit, and that his notion that people who live in bourgeois capitalist societies live in a state of psychological terror has some currency. In our everyday lives, we are under constant "attack" (by print advertisements, radio and television commercials, the programs carried by the mass media) even though we may not recognize that we are being besieged or may not be able to articulate our feelings. (The terrors raised by these attacks may include growing old in a youth-crazed culture, being fat in a thin-crazed culture, being poor in a wealth-obsessed culture, being a person of color in a White-dominated culture, being a woman in a male-dominated culture, always being told or shown that we are suffering from deprivation, whether relative or absolute, and so on, endlessly.)

Whether these pressures we feel (if you don't want to use the word *terror*) are primarily the result of living in complex modern, urban societies or of our specific social, economic, and political arrangements is a question that has yet to be answered. For Lefebvre, the answer is clear.

ALIENATION

The term *alienation* suggests separation and distance; it contains within it the word *alien*, a stranger in a society who has no connections with others, no ties, no "liens" of any sort. This notion is of central importance to an understanding of Marxism, which derives alienation from the capitalist economic system. Capitalism may be able to produce goods and materialist abundance for large numbers of people (although, ultimately, at the expense of others), but it necessarily generates alienation, and all classes suffer from this, whether they recognize it or not.

There is a link between alienation and consciousness. People who live in a state of alienation (or condition of alienation) suffer from "false consciousness"—a consciousness that takes the form of the ideology that dominates their thinking. But in addition to this false consciousness, alienation may be said to be unconscious, in that people do not recognize that they are, in fact, alienated. One reason for this may be that alienation is so all-pervasive that it is invisible and hard to take hold of.

For Fromm and for many other interpreters of Marx, it is alienation that is the core of Marx's theory. As Fromm (1962) has noted:

> The concept of alienation has become increasingly the focus of the discussion of Marx's ideas in England, France, Germany and the U.S.A. . . . The majority of those involved in this debate . . . take a position that alienation and the task of overcoming it is the center of Marx's socialist humanism and the aim of socialism; furthermore that there is a complete continuity between the young and the mature Marx, in spite of changes in terminology and emphasis. (pp. 43-44)

This is a debatable position, Fromm adds. Whatever the case, the concept of alienation is very useful to analysts of popular culture.

The following quotation from Marx (1964) serves to illustrate his views on alienation:

> In what does this alienation of labour consist? First, that the work is *external* to the worker, that it is not a part of his nature, that consequently he does not fulfill himself in his work but denies himself, has a feeling of misery, not of wellbeing, does not develop freely a physical and mental energy, but is physically exhausted and mentally debased. The worker therefore feels himself at home only during his leisure, whereas at work he feels homeless. His work is not voluntary but imposed, *forced labour*. It is not the satisfaction of a need, but only a *means* for satisfying other needs. Its alien character is clearly shown by the fact that as soon as there is no physical or other compulsion it is avoided like the plague. Finally, the alienated character of work for the worker appears in the fact that it is not his work but work for someone else, that in work he does not belong to himself but to another person. . . .
>
> The *alienation* of the worker in his product means not only that his labour becomes an object, takes on its own existence, but that it exists outside him, independently, and alien to him, and that it stands opposed to him as an autonomous power. The life which he has given to the object sets itself against him as an alien and hostile force. (pp. 169-170)

Thus people become separated or estranged from their work, from friends, from themselves, and from life. A person's work, which is central to identity and sense of self, becomes separated from him or her and ends up, actually, as a destructive force. Workers experience themselves as objects, things that are acted upon, and not as subjects, active forces in the world. The things people produce become "commodities," objects separated, somehow, from the workers' labor. As people become increasingly more alienated, they become the prisoners of their alienated needs and end up, as Marx puts it, "the *self-conscious* and *self-acting* commodity" (in Fromm, 1962, p. 51).

In this situation the mass media play a crucial role. They provide momentary gratifications for the alienated spirit, they distract the alienated individual from his or her misery (and from consciousness of the objective facts of his or her situation), and, with the institution of advertising, they stimulate desire, leading people to work harder and harder. There is a kind of vicious cycle here: If, as Marx argues, work in capitalist societies alienates people, then the more people work, the more they become alienated. In order to find some means of escaping their alienation (which they do not recognize as a condition, but the symptoms of which they feel), they engage in various forms of consumption, all of which cost money, so that they are forced to work increasingly hard to escape from the effects of their work. Advertising has replaced the Puritan ethic in America as the chief means of motivating people to work hard; thus advertising must be seen as occupying a central role in advanced capitalist societies.

There is a debate among Marxist critics about the status of Franz Kafka, author of *The Trial, The Castle,* and many other important works. Kafka's writings, critics suggest, show characters struggling with vast, anonymous bureaucracies and reflect the alienation that is so dominant in capitalist societies. The central question many critics argue about is whether it was Kafka's intent to suggest that alienation is a universal condition (and not just tied to capitalism).

Conservative Marxist critics attack Kafka for arguing that alienation is an inevitable condition of human beings and not recognizing that it could be overcome in socialist countries. Kafka did not understand, these critics argue, that alienation is historical, not natural, and he failed to suggest or to show in his stories how alienation might be overcome— through the establishment of socialist societies (i.e., classless ones ruled by communists). Liberal Marxist critics, in contrast, assert that Kafka's work shows that alienation can persist even in socialist countries (which are characterized by enormous bureaucracies), and that it is valuable because it points that out. Kafka's stories make people aware of this alienation, and this ultimately suggests that changes should be made and that alienation can be eradicated.

This critical debate, let me suggest, has been settled by history. The notion that only "socialist realism" is acceptable in art and literature is not taken seriously by many people, nor is "socialist realist" criticism.

THE CONSUMER SOCIETY

Advertising, as I have suggested, is an essential institution in advanced capitalist societies because it is necessary to motivate people to work hard so that they can accumulate money, which they can then use to buy things. But in addition, people must be driven to consume, must be made crazy to consume, for it is consumption that maintains the economic system. Thus the alienation generated by a capitalist system is functional, for the anxieties and miseries generated by such a system tend to be assuaged by impulsive consumption. As Marx has written about the effects of capitalism:

> Every man speculates upon creating a *new* need in another in order to force him to a new sacrifice, to place him in a new dependence, and to entice him into a new kind of pleasure and thereby into economic ruin. Everyone tries to establish over others an *alien* power in order to find there the satisfaction of his own egoistic need. (quoted in Fromm, 1962, p. 50)

Advertising generates anxieties, creates dissatisfactions, and, in general, feeds on the alienation present in capitalist societies to maintain the consumer culture.

There is nothing that advertising will not do, use, or co-opt to achieve its goals. If it has to debase sexuality, co-opt the women's rights movement, merchandise cancer (via cigarettes), seduce children, terrorize the masses, or employ any other tactics, it will. One thing that advertising does is divert people's attention from social and political concerns and steer that attention toward narcissistic and private concerns. Through advertising, individual self-gratification is developed into obsession, and thus alienation is strengthened and the sense of community weakened.

Thus advertising is more than a merchandising tool; it takes control of everyday life and dominates social relationships. At the same time, advertising leads people to turn inward and to separate themselves from one another. It also imposes upon people a collective form of taste. Advertising is a kind of popular art carried by the mass media, an art form that persuades and convinces and thus has an immediate (as well as a long-range) mission. The immediate mission is to sell goods; the long-range mission is to maintain the class system. In order to sell goods, advertising has to change attitudes, lifestyles, customs, habits, and preferences while at the same time maintaining the economic system that benefits from these changes.

Wolfgang Fritz Haug, a German Marxist, has developed a concept that is relevant to this discussion. Haug suggests that those who control the industries in capitalist societies have learned to fuse sexuality onto commodities and thus have gained greater control of that aspect of people's lives that is of most interest to the ruling classes—the purchasing of goods and services. In his book *Critique of Commodity Aesthetics* (1986), Haug argues that the advertising industry, the servant of capitalist interests, has learned how to mold and exploit human sexuality, to alter human need and instinct structures. In his postscript to the eighth German edition of the book, he writes:

> It would be particularly absurd in the case of commodity aesthetics to ignore the fact that its current dominant form is the aesthetics of the monopoly-commodity, i.e., the form in which transnational enterprises in particular intervene directly in the collective imagination of cultures. (p. 11)

Thus this power to use the appearance of products as a means of stimulating desire for them (the aestheticization of commodities) is now a worldwide phenomenon, and people in many different countries are affected by it as it "intervenes" in their cultures by capturing, so to speak, people's imaginations. People have the illusion that they make their own decisions about what to purchase and what to do. According to Haug, to a remarkable degree, these decisions are made for people, whose acts turn out to be almost automatic responses to "stimuli" generated by advertisers and the commodities themselves.

On the cover of *Critique of Commodity Aesthetics* is a remarkable photograph of pigeons in St. Mark's Square in Venice. The photo, taken from a height, shows that the pigeons are arranged so that they spell out *Coca-Cola*. To get this effect, workers scattered birdseed to form the lettering, and the birds flocked to the seed. As Haug explains:

> The pigeons did not gather with the intention of forming the trade-mark but to satisfy their hunger. But equally the seed was not scattered to feed the pigeons but employ them on its tracks as extras. The arrangement is totally alien and external to pigeons. While they are consuming their feed, capital is subsuming, and consuming, them. This picture, a triumph of capitalist advertising technique, symbolizes a fundamental aspect of capitalism. (p. 118)

This photograph is most instructive. We (human beings living in societies dominated by capitalism and commodity aesthetics) are like the pigeons in the photograph; we fly to the things we want to consume under the illusion that we are making individual choices and decisions, whereas in reality we are being motivated and manipulated by forces beyond our control.

In a later book titled *Commodity Aesthetics, Ideology, and Culture* (1987), Haug modified his views somewhat, arguing for a paradigm shift from what was essentially an economistic reading of Marx, which derived ideology, everyday life, and mass culture fairly directly from economic conditions. Haug's new perspective focuses on the development of action "from below" and the capacity people have to resist domination and manipulation in the spheres of culture and economics, which he now sees as separate and distinct.

Nevertheless, the photograph of the pigeons strikes a chord. It shows how our actions can seem motivated purely by personal desire and interest, yet be in reality shaped and controlled by others, for their own purposes. The main instruments of this manipulation of people (as of the pigeons) are advertising and the mass media, along with allied industries such as industrial design.

In his book *The Mechanical Bride* (1967), Marshall McLuhan analyzes advertisements (and comics) as cultural indicators and offers a number of brilliant insights into what specific advertisements reveal about

American culture. In a chapter titled "Love-Goddess Assembly Line," he compares Hollywood and advertising:

> So Hollywood is like the ad agencies in constantly striving to enter and control the unconscious minds of a vast public, not in order to understand it or to present these minds, as the serious novelist does, but in order to exploit them for profit. . . . The ad agencies and Hollywood, in their different ways, are always trying to get inside the public mind in order to impose their collective dreams on that inner stage. (p. 97)

The irony is that we are all convinced of our freedom to make our own choices, because we believe our minds are "inviolable," when in fact our choices are ones that have been imposed upon us, in subtle ways, by the advertising industry. This illusion of autonomy makes us all the more susceptible to manipulation and exploitation.

Advertising is part of what Enzenberger (1974) has called "the consciousness industry" or "the mind industry." In a chapter titled "The Industrialization of the Mind," he has described the ultimate selling job done by advertising and the media:

> The mind industry's main business and concern is not to sell its product: it is to "sell" the existing order, to perpetuate the prevailing pattern of man's domination by man, no matter who runs the society, and by what means. Its main task is to expand and train our consciousness—in order to exploit it. (p. 10)

Advertising can be seen as an industry that uses radical methods for conservative reasons. There is, then, a special irony to the famous phrase used in the advertising industry, "Let's run it up the flagpole and see if anyone salutes." This is meant to be a testimony to advertising's pragmatism and openness to new ideas. What people are "saluting" when they do salute, however, is the old order.

BOURGEOIS HEROES

A great deal of media analysis involves dealing with heroic figures—men, women, animals, robots—who have a number of different functions in films, television series, comic books, commercials, and other dramatic forms. For some people, heroes and heroines—and I am using these terms in the sense of characters who are important (so that villains must also be considered) to dramas and other public art forms—reflect their ages and societies. For others, heroes "shape" their ages and help to transform their societies. In addition, heroes offer people models to imitate and thus help them to attain identities. At times these models are "deviant," so some heroes and heroines disturb whatever equilibrium society has obtained.

For Marxists, bourgeois heroes and heroines function to maintain the status quo by "peddling" capitalist ideology in disguised form and by helping keep consumer lust at a high pitch. One of the ideas bourgeois heroes sell is that of individualism, a value that takes many different forms (the self-made man, the American dream, the "me generation," and so on) but that always is connected to alienation, though few people see the connection. One of the early English Marxists, Christopher Caudwell, discusses heroes in his book *Studies and Further Studies in a Dying Culture* (1971). In his chapter on T. E. Lawrence he writes:

> If any culture produced heroes, it should surely be bourgeois culture. For the hero is an outstanding individual and bourgeoisdom is the creed of individualism. . . . Indeed, bourgeois history, for bourgeois schools, is simply the struggles of heroes with their antagonists and difficulties. (p. 21)

This view of heroism, according to Caudwell, is naive, because it does not recognize that heroes are connected, intimately, to their societies and social and economic phenomena. He continues:

> What is it that constitutes heroism? Personality? No; men with the flattest and simplest personalities have become heroes. Is it courage? A man can do no more than risk and perhaps lose his life, and millions did that in the Great War. Is it success—the utilization of events to fulfill a purpose, something brilliant and dazzling in the execution, a kind of luring and forcing Fortune to obey one, as with that type of all heroes, Julius Caesar? (p. 21)

None of the above is adequate for heroism, for, as Caudwell sees it, heroism is independent of people's motives and is based on the "social significance" of people's acts. The heroes we tend to celebrate are what Caudwell calls "charlatans," who "have power over men but not over matter." Charlatans lack a societal reference and exist as alienated and alienating curiosities. "Society," Marx (1964) has noted, "is not merely an aggregate of individuals; it is the sum of the relations in which these individuals stand to one another" (p. 96). Thus the hero, for the Marxist, is the man or woman who understands this and who fights for a new social order—one in which the bourgeois values of individualism, consumer lust, and upper-class domination are smashed.

HEGEMONY

The concept of hegemony has been described by Raymond Williams (1977) as "one of the major turning points in Marxist cultural theory" (p. 108). In common usage, *hegemony* means domination or rule by one state or nation over another. Marxists use the term in a different manner: Rule is based on overt power and, at times, on coercion, but hegemony is more subtle and more pervasive. As Williams explains, rule is political and, in critical times, is based on coercion or force (p. 108). Hegemony, on the other hand, is a complicated intermeshing of forces of a political, social, and cultural nature. Hegemony transcends (but also includes) two other concepts: culture, which is how we shape our lives, and ideology, which, from a Marxist perspective, expresses and is a projection of specific class interests.

Hegemony transcends culture as a concept because culture can be seen as being tied to "specific distributions of power and influence," or the mode of production and relations that stem from it. And hegemony transcends ideology as a concept because ideology is limited to systematized and formalized meanings that are more or less conscious. Ideology may be masked and camouflaged in films and television programs and other works carried by mass media, but the discerning Marxist can elicit these ideologies and point them out.

This is valuable, but only to a point, because ideological analysis does not cover enough territory, does not lead to the kind of profound analysis that hegemonic analysis makes possible. Williams (1977) explains this as follows, saying about hegemony:

> It is distinct in its refusal to equate consciousness with the articulate
> formal system which can be and ordinarily is abstracted as "ideology."
> It of course does not exclude the articulate and formal meanings,
> values and beliefs which a dominant class develops and propagates.
> But it does not equate these with consciousness, or rather it does not
> reduce consciousness to them. Instead it sees the relations of domi-
> nance and subordination, in their forms as practical consciousness, as
> in effect a saturation of the whole process of living—not only of
> political and economic activity, nor only of manifest social activity, but
> of the whole substance of lived identities and relationships, to such a
> depth that the pressures and limits of what can ultimately be seen as
> a specific economic, political, and cultural system seem to most of us
> the pressures and limits of simple experience and common sense.
> Hegemony is then not only the articulate upper level of "ideology,"
> nor are its forms of control only those ordinarily seen as "manipula-
> tion" or "indoctrination." It is a whole body of practices and expecta-
> tions, over the whole of living: our senses, our assignments of energy,
> our shaping perceptions of ourselves and our world. It is a lived
> system of meanings and values—constitutive and constituting—
> which as they are experienced as practices appear as reciprocally
> confirming. It thus constitutes a sense of reality for most people in the
> society, a sense of the absolute because experienced reality beyond
> which it is very difficult for most members of the society to move, in
> most areas of their lives. (pp. 109-110)

Hegemony thus is what might be described as "that which goes without saying," or the givens or commonsense realities of the world, which, it turns out, serve an ultimate purpose—that of maintaining the dominance of the ruling class.

The works carried by the mass media can be seen, then, not merely as carriers of ideology that manipulate and indoctrinate people with certain views. The media, as unwitting instruments of hegemonic domination, have a much broader and deeper influence—they shape people's very idea of themselves and the world; they shape people's worldviews.

Thus when using the concept of hegemony we must look very deeply into the work we are analyzing and elicit from it not only its ideological content but also its even more fundamental (and perhaps more insidious) ethological, worldview-generating, content. We might think of hegemonic analysis as analogous to the work psychoanalysts do when they probe beneath symptoms to underlying root causes in the personality structure of patients. Williams says that hegemonic analysis is "cultural," but in a special sense, in that it connects culture to the patterns of subordination and domination that exist in a given society.

Let me offer another analogy that might be useful here. The concept of hegemony is similar to that of paradigm, as used by philosophers of science. The term *paradigm* refers to an entire system of thought that characterizes a historical period and plays a major role in shaping the kind of science found in an era. Paradigm shifts occur in science every hundred years or so (or perhaps even less often), and with each paradigm shift, scientists see the world in new ways and work accordingly. The following lists provide a comparison of *hegemony* and *paradigm*:

law	popular arts
theory	ideology
paradigm	hegemony
science	*media analysis*

In both cases, the ultimate determinant of thought and behavior is not recognized, because it is so all-pervasive and fundamental. And just as the theory "explains" the law (or the event in nature that can be explained by law), so the paradigm encompasses all the theories that are held. Likewise, the concept of hegemony encompasses all that exists in a society—ideological notions, works of popular art carried by the media, and so forth. And this makes the analysis of media difficult, because it is hard to put one's finger on all the things one takes for granted and assumes are simply part of reality. We are, all too often, captives of the categories of bourgeois thought—the very thought we hope to expose as the instruments of our own domination.

THE DANGER OF BEING DOCTRINAIRE

Marxism in general, and Marxist media analysis in particular, has a great deal of appeal, especially to people with a strong sense of social justice and a desire for a more egalitarian, more humane world. Despite the awesome complexity that often characterizes Marxist thought, for Marxists the world is basically divided into two camps: the bourgeoisie, who own the instruments of production and are ultimately responsible for alienation and a host of other ills from which all of society suffers, and the proletariat and their allies, who want to save themselves and society. This is a great oversimplification, of course, but it also has a grain of truth; and in any fight between "good guys" and "bad guys," it is only natural to root for the good guys.

In its best form, Marxism is a humanistic system of thought that seeks to make it possible for all people to have productive, useful lives. However, Marxism also is an ideology that explains everything (or nearly everything) in the world on the basis of certain axioms or beliefs from which everything else follows. And that is its danger.

The danger for Marxist media analysts is that they know the answers *before* they ask the questions. That is, Marxists are also prisoners of the categories of their thought, and the questions they ask of a work of popular art carried by the media are often rather limited. Like the proverbial Frenchman (or Freudian) who sees sex in everything, the Marxist media analyst tends to see alienation, manipulation, and ideological exploitation in all of the public arts, and tends to treat art of all kinds primarily in terms of its ideological content. Such analysis is terribly limiting, and cannot do justice to most works of art.

Thus for the Marxist analyst there is a terrible danger of being doctrinaire, of seeing works of popular culture (or anything else) *only* in terms of Marxist concepts and notions. This is not to say that there is no ideological dimension to much or most (or all, many Marxists would argue) of the material produced for the mass media—there is, and media analysts must be mindful of it. But analysts must not neglect other aspects of these works—their psychological, moral, and aesthetic components, for example—and should not attempt to fit the material carried by the media into a Procrustean bed of Marxist notions.

There is also, of course, the possibility that Marx was wrong, and that his notions about the economic system's relation to culture are not correct or are too simplistic to be worth much. There is something destructive about a great deal of utopian idealism, and Marx's fantasies of a communist society may ultimately do a great deal of damage to people who do not recognize that the best is often the enemy of the good. Marx (1964) has written:

For as soon as the division of labor begins, each man has a particular, exclusive sphere of activity, which is forced upon him and from which he cannot escape. He is a hunter, a fisherman, a shepherd, or a critic, and must remain so if he does not want to lose his means of livelihood; whereas in communist society, where nobody has one exclusive sphere of activity, but each can become accomplished in any branch he wishes, production as a whole is regulated by society, thus making it possible for me to do one thing today and another tomorrow, to hunt in the morning, fish in the afternoon, rear cattle in the evening, criticize after dinner, in accordance with my inclination, without ever becoming hunter, fisherman, shepherd or critic. (p. 97)

In the name of achieving this kind of society, however, most of the allegedly socialist Marxist states set up repressive societies in which the media have been used for manipulation much more than they have in Western bourgeois societies. If Marxist media analysts are to be taken seriously as they point out the ways in which soap operas indoctrinate people into bourgeois values and mystify alienated housewives, this is an irony they must explain.

A NOTE ON MARXIST CRITICISM IN THE 1990s

In the first edition of *Media Analysis Techniques*, written in 1982, I suggested that Marxism seemed to have more interesting things to say about culture than about economics. I also pointed out that the Marxist societies that existed were highly repressive and that Marxist critics in the Western world did not see them as role models to which other countries might aspire. Now, with the collapse of communism in Eastern Europe and the Soviet Union, the status of Marxism as a philosophy is being debated. If Marxism was the philosophy that informed (and was used to justify) repressive and totalitarian regimes—dominated all too often, it turns out, by ignorant sociopaths—how much credence can we put in it? Is Marxism dead? If it is not dead, is it dying? At one time, Marxists attacked Western capitalist societies in the name of a higher morality. Marxists argued that though they could not provide people the levels of material comfort found in Western societies, at least the Marxist regimes looked after people and did not exploit them. We now know that in most respects this was a sham.

I realized that communism was dead years ago, when I heard an interesting statistic: Private farms occupied something like 3% of the land in the Soviet Union, yet provided something like 30% of the agricultural products. Marxism, to cut matters short, sounded good but simply didn't work. As the famous joke about work in communist countries goes, "They pretend to pay us and we pretend to work."

What complicates matters is that there are many Marxisms and many different aspects to Marxist thought. As a political philosophy, Marxism now lacks credibility, although it is still the official philosophy of some countries, such as China. How long it will last in those countries remains to be seen. But as a means of criticizing culture, Marxism still seems to have some utility. You don't have to want to set up a society like the ones that existed in Romania or East Germany to be a Marxist, and Marxist cultural criticism—to the extent that it points out how the mass media, and advertising in particular, help shape the consciousness of individuals and societies—can still speak to our moral sensibilities.

It is, I would suggest, the radical egalitarianism in Marxism that makes it appealing to people. Those who use Marxism, in its various incarnations and modernizations, as a tool of social criticism do so in the name of freedom and equality. American Marxists, for the most part, want to establish a more democratic society in the United States; they see Marxism as the philosophy that encompasses the concepts they need to make their criticisms of U.S. society cogent.

Aaron Wildavsky, a distinguished political scientist, has suggested that in modern societies there are four political cultures: hierarchical elitists, competitive individualists, egalitarians, and fatalists. Each of these cultures needs all the others. Wildavsky (1989) has explained how these political cultures come about:

> The dimensions of cultural theory are based on answers to two questions: Who am I? and What shall I do? The question of identity may be answered by saying that individuals belong to a strong group, a collective that makes decisions binding on all members or that their ties are weak in that their choices bind only themselves. The question of action is answered by responding that the individual is subject to many or few prescriptions, a free spirit or a spirit tightly constrained. The strength or weakness of group boundaries and the numerous or

few, varied or similar prescriptions binding or freeing individuals are the components of their culture. (p. 25)

Table 2.1 shows how these political cultures develop out of differences in group boundaries and in the numbers and kinds of prescriptions to which individuals are subject. Some of the beliefs of these groups are sketched out below. (Readers interested in learning more about Wildavsky's theory of political cultures should see his book *Culture Theory*.)

Hierarchical elitists believe in stratification and in the responsibility of those at the top to look after those below them. *Competitive individualists* are interested primarily in themselves, and want the freedom to compete fairly protected by the government. *Egalitarians* stress that people are equal in terms of their needs and that differences between people are social and not natural and should be played down. *Fatalists* believe in luck and opt out of the political system. All four groups are locked into complementary relationships, and all are necessary for the political order.

Egalitarians are critical of hierarchical elitists and competitive individualists (who, according to Wildavsky, form the backbone of democratic societies) and spend a great deal of time championing and trying to raise up the fatalists. It is this egalitarian sensibility that, I would suggest, motivates Marxist culture critics. Egalitarianism, as Seymour Martin Lipset (1979) has pointed out, is one of the core values of American society (along with achievement).

Whether Marxism is the best—or even a credible—philosophy to use as a basis for analyzing and criticizing culture and the mass media is a question that is being debated now. Ironically, it may be that the United States will turn out to be the only place where Marxism is taken seriously.

Ultimately, each of us has to decide for him- or herself whether Marxism makes sense as a basis upon which to analyze the mass media. If an analyst finds the concepts of Marxism useful and believes that they explain things better than other perspectives, that analyst should use them. If not, he or she should approach media analysis from another viewpoint. Philosophies don't really die—they are abandoned when people turn their attention elsewhere. Whether Marxism will be abandoned and dumped on the ash heap of history remains to be seen.

TABLE 2.1 How the Four Political Cultures Develop

Political Culture	Group Boundaries	Numbers and Kinds of Prescriptions
Hierarchical elitists	strong	numerous and varied
Egalitarians	strong	few
Competitive individualists	weak	few
Fatalists	weak	numerous and varied

STUDY QUESTIONS AND TOPICS FOR DISCUSSION

1. What is meant by *dialectical materialism*?
2. Explain how the base relates to the superstructure.
3. What errors do "vulgar Marxists" make?
4. What is an ideology? How are ideologies related to false consciousness?
5. Why are the ideas of the ruling class the ideas of the masses?
6. How do all of the topics raised in questions 1-5 above relate to the matter of class conflict? To alienation? To consumer lust?
7. What are the basic attributes of bourgeois heroes and heroines? How do these heroes differ from Marxist ones?
8. When Marxists do cultural analysis, what do they address?
9. What has been said about advertising in this chapter?
10. What are some of the problems associated with Marxist analysis?

ANNOTATED BIBLIOGRAPHY

Berger, Arthur Asa. (Ed.). (1990). *Agitpop: Political culture and communication theory*. New Brunswick, NJ: Transaction. This volume presents a study of mass media and popular culture as they relate to political culture in the United States.

Berlin, Isaiah. (1963). *Karl Marx: His life and environment*. New York: Galaxy. This is a classic biography of Marx that also explains his ideas and their relation to his experiences.

Caudwell, Christopher. (1971). *Studies and further studies in a dying culture*. New York: Monthly Review Press. In this book a remarkable stylist deals with literary figures, personalities, and concepts. Caudwell's Marxism may be slightly "vulgar," or simplistic, but he has an incredible mind.

Dorfman, Ariel. (1983). *The empire's old clothes: What the Lone Ranger, Babar, and other innocent heroes do to our minds*. New York: Pantheon. Dorfman offers a Marxist critique of such topics as the Lone Ranger, the Babar books, and *Reader's Digest*, arguing that these texts and others are full of ideological messages that spread capitalist ideology and help maintain the status quo.

Eagleton, Terry. (1978). *Criticism and ideology: A study in Marxist theory.* New York: W. W. Norton. Eagleton, a prominent British scholar, offers a Marxist analysis of literary theory that shows its ideological aspects and discusses how texts "produce" ideology.

Enzenberger, Hans Magnus. (1974). *The consciousness industry: On literature, politics and the media.* New York: Seabury. Enzenberger, an influential critic, presents some slightly unorthodox ideas.

Fischer, Ernst. (1963). *The necessity of art: A Marxist approach.* New York: Pelican. This book presents a sophisticated Marxist analysis of art, literature, and aesthetics, with interesting treatment of comics and other elements of popular culture.

Fromm, Erich. (1971). *Beyond the chains of illusion: My encounter with Marx and Freud.* New York: Touchstone. Fromm provides a comparison of the ideas of Marx and Freud that serves as a useful introduction to the thought of both men.

Haug, Wolfgang Fritz. (1986). *Critique of commodity aesthetics: Appearance, sexuality, and advertising in capitalist society.* Minneapolis: University of Minnesota Press. This volume offers a Marxist analysis of the role advertising plays in capitalist societies and the power design has to aestheticize objects and shape consumer behavior.

Haug, Wolfgang Fritz. (1987). *Commodity aesthetics, ideology, and culture.* New York: International General. In this collection of essays written between 1970 and 1983, Haug discusses his theory of commodity aesthetics and applies it to mass culture, workers, and ideology and offers a new paradigm that focuses on what he calls "cultural competence."

Jameson, Fredric. (1991). *Postmodernism; or, The cultural logic of late capitalism.* Durham, NC: Duke University Press. This important book argues that postmodernism is really a form of late capitalism. It addresses, among other things, architecture, film, video, and theoretical matters concerning postmodernism, ideology, and culture.

LeFebvre, Henri. (1984). *Everyday life in the modern world.* New Brunswick, NJ: Transaction. LeFebvre offers a Marxist analysis of everyday life, with important discussions of advertising, fashion, and terror.

Marx, Karl. (1964). *Selected writings in sociology and social philosophy* (T. B. Bottomore and Maximilien Rubel, Eds.; T. B. Bottomore, Trans.). New York: McGraw-Hill, 1964. This is a collection of important passages from Marx's writings, organized and introduced by the editors.

Pappenheim, Fritz. (1959). *The alienation of modern man.* New York: Monthly Review Press. This volume is a wide-ranging study of alienation and its relation to philosophy, literature, technology, and politics, written from a Marxist perspective.

Rius. (1990). *Marx for beginners.* New York: David McKay. This book of cartoons explains the fundamental ideas of Marx and provides a dictionary of Marxist terms; recommended for those who like books with lots of pictures.

Tucker, Robert C. (Ed.). (1972). *The Marx-Engels reader.* New York: W. W. Norton. This volume, edited by one of the foremost scholars of Marxism, provides almost 700 pages of the works of Marx and Engels, showing the evolution of their thought.

Williams, Raymond. (1977). *Marxism and literature.* Oxford: Oxford University Press. Williams, an influential British Marxist, addresses culture and literature. The book includes a useful bibliography of Marxist texts.

Psychoanalysis is a therapeutic technique, but it is also a form of inquiry that has been applied to many areas—politics, anthropology, and literary criticism, to name a few. It yields interesting results, but results that are also generally controversial. This chapter explores the most significant aspects of psychoanalytic theory and shows how the principles of psychoanalytic thought can be used to explain the hidden significance of cigarette lighters and <u>Hamlet</u>, among other things.

CHAPTER 3

Psychoanalytic Criticism

THE UNCONSCIOUS

Psychoanalytic criticism is a form of applied psychoanalysis, a science concerned with the interaction of conscious and unconscious processes and with the laws of mental functioning. It should not be confused with psychotherapy, which is concerned with treating mental illness and behavioral problems, though many psychotherapists use various kinds of analysis in their work. Rather, psychoanalytic criticism is one of many different forms of study that use psychoanalytic concepts to understand particular subject matter. Thus there are psychoanalytically inclined sociologists, anthropologists, and political scientists, as well as critics, and all of them use concepts and insights from psychoanalytic theory in their work.

Freud did not discover the unconscious; Plato, Nietzsche, Bergson, and many others discussed it before Freud. However, Freud developed the concept most thoroughly, and it is with Freud that all neo-Freudians, post-Freudians, anti-Freudians, and non-Freudians must come to grips. He was a seminal thinker of incredible power and scope, and his ideas and insights have fueled the work of generations of scholars in numerous fields. What I will offer in this section is not a full-scale explication of Freudian thought, but a selection of some of his most important concepts—concepts that can be applied to the media to help clarify how they work and how they affect us. Freud was most interested in helping people, but in the course of his amazing career he wrote on many other subjects, such as folklore, humor, and theater—pointing the way toward the development of psychoanalytic criticism.

One of the keystones in psychoanalytic theory is the concept of the unconscious. As Freud writes in his essay "Psychoanalysis" (1963):

> It was a triumph for the interpretative art of psychoanalysis when it succeeded in demonstrating that certain common mental acts of normal people, for which no one had hitherto attempted to put forward a psychological explanation, were to be regarded in the same light as the symptoms of neurotics: that is to say they had a *meaning*, which was unknown to the subject but which could easily be discovered by analytic means. . . . A class of material was brought to light which is calculated better than any other to stimulate a belief in the existence of unconscious mental acts even in people to whom the hypothesis of something at once mental and unconscious seems strange and even absurd. (pp. 235-236)

We are not, then, aware of everything that is going on in our minds. Not only that, we are aware of only a little that is going on in our minds— only a small portion of our mental lives is accessible to us.

It has frequently been suggested that an individual's mental life can be represented by an iceberg. The tip of the iceberg, that part seen above the water, is what the person is conscious of. The remainder of the iceberg, by far the greater part of it, lies hidden beneath the water. Though it is not seen, it is still there. "What is in your mind," Freud (1963) has noted, "is not identical with what you are conscious of; whether something is going on in your mind and whether you hear of it, are two different things" (p. 189).

This means that we are not in complete control of ourselves all the time, we are affected in ways we cannot fathom, and we do things for reasons we do not understand or will not admit to ourselves. In short, we are not completely rational creatures who act only on the basis of logic and intelligence, but instead are vulnerable to emotional and other kinds of nonrational or irrational appeals.

But why, you may ask, don't we become conscious of all that is going on in our minds? Why does all this material elude us? Why do our minds play such tricks on us? Freud offers an explanation that is both obvious (once it is pointed out) and ingenious: We *repress* this material because we do not want, for a variety of reasons, to become conscious of it. It would cause us pain or guilt or some other unpleasant feeling. Thus we create a barrier between our consciousness and our unconscious and do not allow repressed material to pass through that barrier.

Ernest Dichter is one of the founding fathers of the field known as motivation research. The goal of motivation research is to discover the unconscious or, it is assumed, real reasons that people do things, so that manufacturers and others can better shape people's behavior—that is, get them to buy particular products or do whatever else is asked of them. In *The Strategy of Desire* (1960), Dichter writes:

> Whatever your attitude toward modern psychology or psychoanalysis, it has been proved beyond any doubt that many of our daily decisions are governed by motivations over which we have no control and of which we are often quite unaware. (p. 12)

Dichter and other motivation researchers, then, "mine" the unconscious and put it to work, so to speak.

Dichter (1964) offers an example of the way in which unconscious desires and forces operate in a discussion of cigarette lighters:

> The reliability of a lighter is important because it is integrally connected with the basic [read "unconscious"] reason for using a lighter. (p. 341)

Let me interrupt here to ask what you think this "basic reason" might be. The answer most people would give would be, "That's obvious—to light cigarettes." But that is the conscious, or "manifest," reason. The basic, or "real," reason and the "latent" and unconscious reason are sometimes entirely different.

Let us return to Dichter (1964), who tells us why people use lighters:

> The basic reason for using a lighter [is] . . . the desire for mastery and power. The capacity to summon fire inevitably gives every human being, child or grownup, a sense of power. Reasons go far back into man's history. Fire and the ability to command it are prized because they are associated not only with warmth, but also with life itself. As attested to by the Greek legend of Prometheus and many other myths,

the ability to control fire is an age-old symbol of man's conquest of the physical world he inhabits.

A cigarette lighter provides conspicuous evidence of this ability to summon fire. The ease and speed with which the lighter works enhances the feeling of power. The failure of a lighter to work does not just create superficial social embarrassment, it frustrates a deep-seated desire for a feeling of mastery and control. (p. 341)

Thus cigarette lighters are important to people because lighters fulfill powerful but unconscious needs and desires. The same can be said of many of the films we see, television programs we watch, novels we read, and other art forms we find so necessary to our lives. All of these things feed our unconscious lives, our psyches, in ways that few people understand.

But the need for mastery and power is only part of the story, for at a deeper level there is something else connected with the humble cigarette lighter. Dichter explains:

Research evidence suggests that at a still deeper level the need for certainty that a cigarette lighter will work matters as much as it does because it is also bound up with the idea of sexual potency. The working of the lighter becomes a kind of symbol of the flame which must be lit in consummating sexual union. (p. 341)

This leads us to our next important subject—sexuality. Many people are aware that Freud was interested in sexuality, but know little more than that. And often the little knowledge they have of Freud's views is simplistic, which leads to absurd misconceptions.

SEXUALITY

Many people are negative or even hostile toward Freud's work because of his views on sexuality. However, I believe that much of this hostility is based in misunderstanding of Freud's theories, and also that it is related, in the United States at least, to extreme sensitivity to the topic of sexuality. Americans resist intrusion into this most private and personal aspect of our lives and may even repress—refuse to admit to consciousness—ideas and insights that would explain sexuality in general and our behavior in particular.

Freud calls the "force by which the sexual instinct is represented in the mind" the *libido*. This term should be understood broadly, and not as being restricted only to sexual relations; that is, *libido* refers to various kinds of sensual pleasures and gratifications. According to Freud, all individuals pass through four stages in their development: the oral, the anal, the phallic, and the genital. In *The Encyclopedia of Psychoanalysis* these stages are described as follows:

> The mouth represents an erotogenic zone for the infant. Sucking and later eating represent the gratification of oral needs. The fact that the infant often sucks a pacifier indicates that he is not only concerned with the incorporation of calories. When the infant begins to have teeth, the need to bite expresses his sadistic desires. The second stage of development is usually referred to as the sadistic-anal, and is characterized by the infant's interest in excreting or retaining his stools. Finally, the third stage is referred to as the phallic, in which the boy is interested in his penis and the girl in her clitoris. The boy's interest in his penis appears to be responsible for his positive Oedipus complex, which is finally dissolved by the fear of castration. The girl reacts with penis envy, if she considers her clitoris to be an inferior organ to the penis.
>
> Freud pointed out that the stages are not clear-cut, and that the fourth stage, the genital phase, is achieved only with puberty. (Eidelberg, 1968, pp. 210-211)

During infancy and childhood, an individual's sexual life is rich, but dissociated and unfocused. Focusing occurs at puberty.

One of the difficulties in explaining psychoanalytic theory is that one seems to have to know everything at the same time. In the above quotation, for example, a number of concepts are mentioned that might need a bit of amplification, such as the matter of anality, the Oedipus complex, and the related concepts of castration anxiety and penis envy. These concepts are difficult for many people to accept and often strike those who are unfamiliar with Freud and psychoanalytic thought as fantastic and farfetched. Perhaps it is most useful to think of all of the above-named as concepts that Freud developed to explain the phenomena and behaviors he encountered in his work. He has described psychoanalysis as "always incomplete and always ready to correct or modify its theories" (1963, p. 251).

Let us start with the matter of anal behavior, or what Freud calls "anal eroticism" in a fascinating paper titled "Character and Anal Eroticism." Freud connects a combination of personality traits that have developed to an extreme degree—orderliness, parsimoniousness, and obstinacy—with people who have had problems overcoming their anal stage, and who may use these personality traits as a means of dealing with it. What is most fascinating is that there are "connections which exist between the two complexes of interest in money and of defecation, which seem so dissimilar" that are, or appear to be, "most far-reaching." Freud (1963) writes:

> In reality, wherever archaic modes of thought predominate or have persisted—in ancient civilizations, in myth, fairy-tale and superstition, in unconscious thoughts and dreams, and in the neuroses— money comes into the closest relation with excrement. We know how the money which the devil gives his paramours turns to excrement after his departure, and the devil is most certainly nothing more than a personification of the unconscious instinctual forces. (p. 31)

Ultimately there is an identification of gold with feces, "the most precious substance known to man and the most worthless" (p. 32).

THE OEDIPUS COMPLEX

The Oedipus complex represents the core of neurosis for Freud; it is a concept that explains a great deal. In a famous letter that Freud wrote on October 15, 1897, to Wilhelm Fliess, he described how he came to recognize the existence and importance of the Oedipus complex:

> Being entirely honest with oneself is a good exercise. Only one idea of general value has occurred to me. I have found love of the mother and jealousy of the father in my own case too, and now believe it to be a general phenomena of early childhood, even if it does not always occur so early as in children who have been made hysterics. . . . If that is the case, the gripping power of *Oedipus Rex*, in spite of all the rational objections to the inexorable fate that the story presupposes, becomes intelligible, and one can understand why later fate dramas were such

failures. Our feelings rise against any arbitrary individual fate . . . but the Greek myth seizes on a compulsion which everyone recognizes because he has felt traces of it in himself. Every member of the audience was once a budding Oedipus in fantasy, and this dream-ful-fillment played out in reality causes everyone to recoil in horror, with the full measure of repression which separates his infantile from his present state.

The idea has passed through my head that the same thing may lie at the root of *Hamlet*. I am not thinking of Shakespeare's conscious intentions, but supposing rather that he was impelled to write it by a real event because his own unconscious understood that of his hero. How can one explain the hysteric Hamlet's phrase "So conscience doth make cowards of us all," and his hesitation to avenge his father by killing his uncle, when he himself so casually sends his courtiers to their death and despatches Laertes so quickly? How better than by the torment roused in him by the obscure memory that he himself had meditated the same deed against his father because of passion for his mother—"use every man after his desert, and who should scape whipping?" His conscience is his unconscious feeling of guilt. (quoted in Grotjahn, 1966, pp. 84-85)

According to psychoanalytic theory, every individual passes through a stage in which he or she desires the parent of the opposite sex—all of this, of course, on an unconscious level. Most people learn to master their Oedipus complexes; neurotic individuals are plagued by them. In little boys this mastery is aided by an unconscious fear of castration—castration anxiety—and in little girls it is aided by jealousy of men and what is termed penis envy.

Little boys, according to Freudian theory, sexualize their love for their mothers and wish to displace their fathers and monopolize their mothers' affection. Their fear of retaliation by their fathers then leads them to renounce their love of their mothers, to identify with the masculinity of their fathers, to rechannel their love outside of the family, and to direct their interest toward other females.

With little girls, the situation is different. They do not have to fear castration (some theorists suggest that they believe they have already lost their penises) and so do not relinquish their Oedipal desires as quickly as boys do. But girls do fear the loss of the love of both their parents, and so avoid this loss by reidentifying with their mothers and turning, eventually, to males other than their fathers as a means of obtaining babies (and, indirectly, their lost penises).

Freud also wrote about several other related complexes that are of interest here. For example, the *Heracles complex* is characterized by a hatred of the father for his children. The father sees the children as rivals for the affection of the wife, and so wishes to get rid of the children. The *Jocasta complex* (named for the mother of Oedipus) is characterized by abnormal attachment of the mother to her son; it is found in varying degrees of intensity, from simple overattachment to incestuous relations.

One of the ways in which young children deal with their Oedipal anxieties is through exposure to fairy tales. In *The Uses of Enchantment* (1977), Bruno Bettelheim devotes a chapter to Oedipal conflicts and resolutions in which he argues that fairy tales can help children to resolve these problems. Children identify with the heroes and heroines of such stories and learn important things about life as well. Fairy tales, Bettelheim suggests, speak to children indirectly and symbolically—the stories are often about some unlikely hero who "proves himself by slaying dragons, solving riddles, and living by his wits and goodness until eventually he frees the beautiful princess, marries her, and lives happily ever after" (p. 111). In stories that speak to little girls, there is usually some evil stepmother or enchantress who is intensely jealous of the heroine and tries to prevent some hero, such as Prince Charming, from finding his princess. Sometimes in these tales the mother is split into two characters—an evil stepmother and a good mother (or fairy godmother).

Fairy tales are important because they help children cope with the psychological difficulties they experience. As Bettelheim (1977) explains:

> Through the centuries (if not millennia) during which, in their retelling, fairy tales became ever more refined, they came to convey at the same time overt and covert meanings—came to speak simultaneously to all levels of the human personality, communicating in a manner which reaches the uneducated mind of the child as well as that of the sophisticated adult. Applying the psychoanalytic model of the human personality, fairy tales carry important messages to the conscious, preconscious and unconscious mind, on whatever level each is functioning at the time. By dealing with universal human problems, particularly those which preoccupy the child's mind, these stories speak to his budding ego and encourage its development, while at the same

time relieving preconscious and unconscious pressures. As the stories unfold, they give conscious credence and body to id pressures and show ways to satisfy these that are in line with ego and superego requirements. (pp. 5-6)

Fairy tales, as well as other texts that are very much like fairy tales (and may be, in truth, modernized fairy tales), have important functions as far as our psyches are concerned.

I cannot resist pointing out in passing that the relationship between Luke Skywalker and Darth Vader in *Star Wars* is (we eventually discover) an Oedipal one. *Star Wars* is, to a great degree, a modernized fairy tale about a princess in distress and a young man who rescues her. There are many other kinds of elements in the film as well—Germanic villains and World War II airplane battles, for example—but the core of the film is, I would suggest, a fairy tale.

We must keep in mind that all of the phenomena discussed in this section operate beyond our consciousness and are kept buried through our power to resist and repress things that would disturb us. We empathize with Hamlet and with countless other heroes and heroines because, unconsciously, we recognize that their battles are our battles and their difficulties are our difficulties.

ID, EGO, AND SUPEREGO

The id, ego, and superego are part of what is usually referred to as Freud's *structural* hypothesis about mental functioning. Charles Brenner (1974) offers the following brief description of these three phenomena:

We may say that id comprises the psychic representatives of the drives, the ego consists of those functions which have to do with the individual's relation to his environment, and the superego comprises the moral precepts of our minds as well as our ideal aspirations.

The drives, of course, we assume to be present from birth, but the same is certainly not true of interest in or control of the environment on the one hand, nor of any moral sense or aspirations on the other. It is obvious that neither of the latter, that is neither the ego nor the superego develops till sometime after birth.

Freud expressed this fact by assuming that the id comprised the entire psychic apparatus at birth, and that the ego and superego were

originally parts of the id which differentiated sufficiently in the course
of growth to warrant their being considered as separate functional
entities. (p. 38)

Each of these entities—the id, ego, and superego—is extremely complicated, and Freud and others have written a great deal about how each
develops and functions, and the importance of each to the individual's
psychic life.

Freud's structural hypothesis superseded his earlier theory of mental functioning, known as the *topographic*, which divided the psyche into
three systems: conscious, preconscious, and unconscious. (I have dealt
with these notions already, although I left out the preconscious in order
to simplify matters.) In essence, according to the structural hypothesis
the psyche is in constant struggle, as the id and superego war against
one another. The poor ego tries to mediate between the two—between
the desire for pleasure and the fear of punishment, between the drives
and the conscience.

Freud's description of the id in his *New Introductory Lectures on
Psychoanalysis* is most graphic:

> We can come nearer to the id with images, and call it chaos, a cauldron
> of seething excitement. We suppose that it is somewhere in direct
> contact with somatic processes, and takes over from them instinctual
> needs and gives them mental expression, but we cannot say in what
> substratum this contact is made. These instincts fill it with energy, but
> it has no organization and no unified will, only an impulsion to obtain
> satisfaction for the instinctual needs, in accordance with the pleasure-
> principle. (quoted in Hinsie & Campbell, 1970, p. 372)

This bubbling cauldron of sexual desire, passion, lust, and desire must
not be allowed to determine an individual's actions, because we live in
societies, and civilization demands that we control our behavior. In fact,
the demands that civilization makes on us are so great, according to
Freud (1962), that we suffer from great psychological pain.

The superego corresponds, as Brenner (1974) notes, "in a general
way to what we ordinarily call conscience. It comprises the moral
functions of the personality." He lists the functions of the superego:

1. the approval or disapproval of actions and wishes on the grounds of rectitude. 2. critical self-observation. 3. self-punishment. 4. the demand for reparation or repentance of wrong-doing. 5. self-praise or self-love as a reward for virtuous or desirable thoughts and actions. Contrary to the ordinary meaning of "conscience," however, we understand that the functions of the superego are often largely or completely unconscious. (pp. 111-112)

The superego assumes, then, a position in opposition to the id. In between these two polarities, the ego tries to mediate, operating always with the aim of self-preservation. The ego carries out its function by storing up experiences in the memory, avoiding excessively strong stimuli through flight, adapting to moderately strong stimuli, and bringing about changes in the world through activity.

We can use the concepts of the id, ego, and superego to help us understand texts. In certain texts, characters may be seen as primarily id figures or ego figures or superego figures. For example, in *Star Trek*, I would suggest that Spock is, essentially, an ego figure, Kirk (in German, interestingly, the name means "church") is a superego figure, and McCoy is an id figure. Spock, the emotionless Vulcan, represents pure rationality. Kirk, the commander of the *Enterprise*, more or less determines what it is to be done, and so represents the superego. And McCoy, who is very emotional and often operates on the basis of his feelings, represents the id.

In some texts it is easy to identify characters as id, ego, or superego figures. Superman, Dick Tracy, Luke Skywalker, and countless other heroes and heroines and caped crusaders are obviously superego figures. But others, such as James Bond and Indiana Jones, are more complicated; they may be more id and ego figures, perhaps, than superego ones. Villains, of course, are almost always id figures; they lack superego development and are interested only in gratifying their desires. They may be intelligent and shrewd, but they lack a sense of right and wrong.

We can also examine various genres in terms of the Freudian structural hypothesis. Certain kinds of films and television programs, such as news shows, interview programs, and documentaries, can be classified as essentially ego texts. Texts that feature the police or that have religious messages are obviously superego texts. And soap operas and other television programs and films that involve sexuality (video pornography, MTV) tend to be id texts. It is not always possible to label a text as clearly representing id, ego, or superego, but in some cases, especially when the work is a formulaic one, it does make sense.

SYMBOLS

Psychoanalysis is, remember, an interpretive art. It seeks to find meaning in the behavior of people and in the arts they create. One way we can apply psychoanalytic theory is by understanding how the psyche works and learning how to interpret the hidden significance of what people and characters in fictions do. We ask ourselves questions, such as, "What does it mean when Hamlet says this or that?" or "What does it mean when Hamlet is unable to act?" We want to know *why.*

This is where symbols come in. Symbols are things that stand for other things, many of which are hidden or at least not obvious. A symbol can stand for an institution, a mode of thought, an idea, a wish—any number of things. Heroes and heroines are often symbolic and thus can be interpreted in terms of all the things they stand for. And much of what is most interesting about symbols is their relation to the unconscious. Symbols are keys that enable us to unlock the doors shielding our unconscious feelings and beliefs from scrutiny. Symbols are messages from our unconscious.

Hinsie and Campbell (1970) define symbolism as follows:

> The act or process of representing an order or idea by a substitute object, sign, or signal. In psychiatry, symbolism is of particular importance since it can serve as a defense mechanism of the ego, as where unconscious (and forbidden) aggressive or sexual impulses come to expression through symbolic representation and thus are able to avoid censorship. (p. 734)

According to this theory, then, we mask our unconscious sexual and aggressive desires through symbolization, which enables us to escape guilt from the superego.

Interpreting symbols can involve a number of difficulties. (I might point out that there are many different theories in psychology about symbols, and they have, like many other aspects of psychoanalytic thought, generated a great deal of controversy.) First, symbols are often ambivalent and can be explained in varying ways depending upon one's orientation. For instance, some people see Hamlet's inability to act as symbolic of the power of an unresolved Oedipus complex, whereas others believe that it symbolizes his skepticism and overintellectualism. Some think that Hamlet is paralyzed by grief; others think he is insane. (If you are interested in the "problem" of Hamlet, I recommend that you read *Hamlet and Oedipus*, by Ernest Jones [1949]. Jones provides a fascinating, though doctrinaire Freudian, interpretation of this symbolic hero.)

Symbols may be classified as conventional, accidental, and universal. *Conventional* symbols are words that we learn that stand for things. In contrast to these are *accidental* symbols, which are personal, private, and connected to an individual's life history. For example, for a man who fell in love for the first time in Paris, Paris may become an accidental symbol for love. (The accidental symbols found in dreams are what make the interpretation of dreams so complicated, though dreams contain more than accidental symbols.) Finally, *universal* symbols are those that are rooted in the experience of all people. Many of these are connected to our bodies and to natural processes. Attempting to understand symbols is often complicated by the fact that the logic behind symbolization is frequently not the same logic that people use in their everyday reasoning processes.

A broad comparison can be drawn between dreams and the works carried by the mass media. For a long time, neither were considered very important; neither dreams nor the texts of the media were thought to have any effects upon us, and so neither attracted much serious attention. Now we know better. Dreams tend to be visual, so they are best compared to such media as film, television, and the comics. And just as dreams can be interpreted through analysis of their symbolic content, so can the mediated dreams that we find in the cinema or on the television screen. In both cases we ask the same questions: What is going on? What disguises are there? What gratifications do we get? What do the various symbolic heroes and heroines tell us about ourselves and our societies?

DEFENSE MECHANISMS

Defense mechanisms are the various techniques employed by the ego to control instincts and ward off anxieties. All of us make use of these mechanisms from time to time, though we are seldom conscious of doing so. In like manner, much of what the media bring us involves human beings in varying kinds of relationships, so many of the characters we see or read about can be interpreted (often) in terms of their defense mechanisms. That is, their behavior may make more sense to us if we can relate it to the defenses people use to maintain their equilibrium. We can also understand our fascination with mass media in terms of defense mechanisms.

Following is a list of some of the most important defense mechanisms, with a brief description of each:

- *Ambivalence:* A simultaneous feeling of love and hate or attraction and repulsion toward the same person or object. Sometimes these feelings alternate in rapid succession in people who wish to be able to gratify contradictory wishes.
- *Avoidance:* Refusal to become involved with subjects that are distressing because they are connected to unconscious sexual or aggressive impulses.
- *Denial or disavowal:* Refusal to accept the reality of something that generates anxiety by blocking it from consciousness or by becoming involved in a wish-fulfilling fantasy.
- *Fixation:* Obsessive preoccupation or attachment to something, generally the result of some traumatic experience.
- *Identification:* The desire to become "like" someone or something in some aspect of thought or behavior.
- *Projection:* An attempt to deny some negative or hostile feeling in oneself by attributing it to someone else. Thus a person who hates someone will "project" that hatred onto another, and perceive that person as being the one who hates.
- *Rationalization:* The offering of logical reasons or excuses for behavior generated by unconscious and irrational determinants. (This term was introduced into psychoanalysis by Ernest Jones.)
- *Reaction formation:* This occurs when a pair of ambivalent attitudes generates problems, so one element is suppressed and kept unconscious by overemphasis on the other (its opposite), though it doesn't disappear. For example, a person might have ambivalent feelings of love and hatred

toward another; the hate may be made unconscious and kept unconscious by an overemphasis on love, so that it appears to be replaced by love.

✔ *Regression:* The return to an earlier stage in life development when confronted with a stressful or anxiety-provoking situation.

✔ *Repression:* The barring from consciousness of unconscious instinctual wishes, memories, desires, and the like. This is considered the most basic defense mechanism.

✔ *Suppression:* The purposeful putting out of the mind and consciousness something that the individual finds painful. This is the second most basic defense mechanism. (Because suppression is voluntary, suppressed material can be recalled to consciousness fairly easily, unlike repressed material, which is very difficult to bring to consciousness.)

Let me suggest how a media analyst might apply knowledge of defense mechanisms by presenting an example involving regression. In an analysis that I conducted some years ago, I contrasted Pac-Man with other video games that preceded it, such as Space Invaders. For more than a year, Pac-Man was the most popular video game in the United States, which is one of the reasons I analyzed it.

In Space Invaders, players fly through the open skies, zapping invading aliens. Two things about Space Invaders are important to this analysis: First, there is freedom to fly about; second, the game is phallic. In Pac-Man, on the other hand, the play is restricted to an enclosed area and the "attacks" involve eating. In other words, aggression in Pac-Man is oral. What we have in Pac-Man, then, is a regression from the phallic (guns) to the oral (biting) as a means of fighting and a change from the freedom to race around the skies to confinement in a maze. From a developmental perspective, Pac-Man is regressive.

The significance of this regression raises interesting questions. When it is not pathological, regression often involves an attempt to escape from anxiety of some kind and is a perfectly normal kind of behavior that functions "in the service of the ego." It may be that the popularity of Pac-Man suggested that, somehow, large numbers of American young people (though they were not the only ones playing it) were experiencing anxieties, and that they were using to game to assuage those anxieties. Curiously, there is often a connection between regression and fixation, so the fact that so many people played the game over and over again should not be too surprising.

Regression and all of the other defense mechanisms listed above are concepts that can be applied to the behavior of characters in films, television programs, and other texts and to various other aspects of the media. These concepts can help us to understand human motivation and can enrich and deepen our ability to analyze the media.

Defense mechanisms are functions of the ego, which uses them against the id. When the id threatens the ego, generating anxiety, the ego uses whatever it can to neutralize the id. There is a considerable amount of disagreement among psychoanalysts as to what can legitimately be called defense mechanisms (there are other techniques the ego has for mastering the id), but the ones listed above are generally accepted as the most important.

DREAMS

It is possible, without stretching things too much, to make a comparison between dreams and many of the fictions brought to us by the media—especially the moving-image media, such as film and television. Dreams are like films and television productions in that they are made up of images, generally have a narrative structure (though it may be obscure and bizarre), and are frequently hard to fathom. According to Erich Fromm (1957):

> Dreams are understood to be the hallucinatory fulfillment of irrational wishes and particularly sexual wishes which have originated in our early childhood and have not been fully transformed into reaction formations or sublimations. These wishes are expressed as being fulfilled when our conscious control is weakened, as is the case in sleep. (p. 67)

The situation is complicated by the fact that we don't allow ourselves to dream about certain things, which implies that some kind of a censoring agent is at work that prevents certain forbidden thoughts to appear undisguised. This is where symbols (which we've already discussed) come in—they allow us to sneak "forbidden" material past our internal censors. Most of these symbols are sexual, as Fromm points out:

> The male genital is symbolized by sticks, trees, umbrellas, knives, pencils, hammers, airplanes, and many other objects which represent it either by their shape or by their function. The female genital is represented in the same manner by caves, bottles, boxes, doors, jewel cases, gardens, flowers, etc. Sexual pleasure is represented by activities like dancing, riding, climbing, flying. The falling out of hair or teeth is a symbolic representation of castration. Aside from sexual elements, symbols are expressive of the fundamental experiences of the little child. Father and mother are symbolized by king and queen or emperor and empress, children as little animals, death as a journey. (pp. 68-69)

This is one part of Freudian theory that often strikes people as ridiculous, and it has given Freud and psychoanalytic theory a bad name in many circles. However, Freud is often disparaged for this aspect of his theory by people who have not read his work at all, or who have read very little of it. To the average person, and to many others who have read a little in the field, the idea of seeing pencils and cigars as penises is simply absurd. One of the nice things about psychoanalytic theory is that this kind of behavior can be explained as repression—the refusal to acknowledge one's sexuality and other aspects of the psyche.

Many of Freud's critics take comfort in quoting a statement that has been attributed to him: "Sometimes a cigar is just a cigar." They generally employ this remark when someone else has used a Freudian interpretation of symbols to describe some object or artifact as a phallic symbol. I once suggested that the Washington monument, a great shaft erected in honor of the *father* of our country, is quite obviously a phallic symbol—though I don't believe that the people responsible for the monument thought of it as such. "Ha!" replied a critic, who then offered the cigar quote.

My point here is that if sometimes a cigar is just a cigar, other times a cigar is *not* just a cigar. You can't have it both ways. The notion that certain objects represent, to the unconscious mind, penises (and other objects, of course, represent vaginas or wombs) may strike you as absurd, but if you are going to argue that suggesting something is a phallic symbol is incorrect in some cases, you must accept the notion that in other cases, suggesting something is a phallic symbol may be correct.

In any case, dreams require interpretation, and that interpretation must be keyed to the dreamer's life. The dreamer can help an analyst to discover a dream's true meaning by participating in free association—revealing all the thoughts that come into his or her mind—and by restructuring the dream. Fromm (1957) writes:

> This true dream, which is the expression of our hidden desires, Freud calls the "latent dream." The distorted version of the dream as we remember it is the "manifest dream" and the process of distortion and disguise is the "dream-work." The main mechanisms through which the dream-work translates the latent into the manifest dream are condensation, displacement and secondary elaboration. By condensation Freud refers to the fact that the manifest dream is much shorter than the latent dream. It leaves out a number of elements of the latent dream, combines fragments of various elements, and condenses them into one new element in the manifest dream. . . . By displacement Freud refers to the fact that an element of the latent dream, and often a very important one, is expressed by a remote element in the manifest dream and usually one which appears to be quite unimportant. (pp. 69-70)

The process of secondary elaboration involves filling in gaps in the dream, repairing inconsistencies, and so on, so the manifest dream *seems* consistent and coherent. Two things make analyzing dreams especially difficult: the fact that elements in dreams often stand for their opposites, and the fact that the manifest dream is not a coherent narrative but a series of disconnected images. Thus a dream represents a formidable problem to the analyst, who must understand how dreams disguise and distort things and be able to relate what is found in dreams to the dreamer's personal life.

Jacques Lacan, a French thinker, has suggested that the semiotic concepts of metaphor and metonymy are useful for understanding dreams. Condensation, according to Lacan, is similar to what I have described in Chapter 1 of this volume as metaphor, and displacement is similar to metonymy. In condensation and in metaphor, we tie concepts together; in displacement and in metonymy, we substitute one thing for something else. Lacan (1966) differs with Freud over the nature of the unconscious. According to Freud, the unconscious is chaotic and preverbal, whereas Lacan argues that "the unconscious is structured like a language," which suggests that semiotics and linguistics might be useful in understanding how the unconscious works.

Recently, some researchers have suggested that Freud's theories about dreams being responses to experiences and being based on wish fulfillment might be inadequate. Whatever the case, his notions about how dreams function and the roles that condensation and displacement play in dreams have interesting implications for the study of how the media affect individuals and, through individuals, society.

As I have noted above, many of the products of the mass media can be viewed as similar to dreams—in analyzing these products, we must look for distortions and disguises, we must concern ourselves with the unconscious and with censorship, and we must relate what we discover in mediated works to the personal histories of the dreamers (which involve both their biographies and their social situations). We must also recognize the influences of the psyches of the creators and interpreters of these works. Clearly, the situation is quite complicated.

We can assume that apart from the surface communication between the artist/creator and the audience/receiver, there is also communication from the subconscious or unconscious of one to that of the other, so that some of the most important aspects of what we get from media may be submerged and not readily observable. This is why knowledge of the psyche and how it functions is so important.

AGGRESSION AND GUILT

In *Civilization and Its Discontents* (1962), one of his last books, Freud discusses aggressiveness in people:

> Men are not gentle creatures who want to be loved, and who at the most can defend themselves if they are attacked; they are, on the contrary, creatures among whose instinctual endowments is to be reckoned a powerful share of aggressiveness. As a result, their neigh-

bor is for them not only a potential helper or sexual object, but also
someone who tempts them to satisfy their aggressiveness on him, to
exploit his capacity for work without compensation, to use him sexually without his consent, to seize his possessions, to humiliate him, to
cause him pain, to torture and to kill him. *Homo homini lupus* [Man is
a wolf to man]. (p. 58)

In this passage Freud suggests that aggressiveness is instinctual, but
secondary to more basic instincts, as his use of the phrase "a powerful
share" indicates. This aggressiveness could threaten to disrupt or even
destroy society and civilization as we know it, so a powerful opposing
force is brought into play. This force is guilt, which, Freud (1962)
explains, is aggression turned back on itself:

Another question concerns us. . . . What means does civilization employ in order to inhibit the aggressiveness which opposes it, to make
it harmless, to get rid of it, perhaps? . . . [Man's] aggressiveness is
introjected, internalized; it is, in point of fact, sent back to where it
came from—that is, it is directed toward his own ego. There is taken
over by a portion of the ego, which sets itself over against the rest of
the ego as super-ego, and which now, in the form of "conscience," is
ready to put into action against the ego the same harsh aggressiveness
that the ego would like to satisfy upon other, extraneous individuals. . . . Civilization, therefore, obtains mastery of the individual's
dangerous desire for aggression by weakening and disarming it and
by setting up an agency within him to watch over it, like a garrison in
a conquered city. (pp. 70-71)

In fact, Freud argues, we are made to feel so guilty that at times we
become overwhelmed with guilt and forfeit our sense of happiness. The
"cost" of civilization is generally too great for us; we are forced to
renounce too much (especially our sexuality), and we suffer from too
much guilt.

This is where humor comes in, for in humor we have developed a
way to allow ourselves to enjoy certain kinds of aggression by masking
them and thus evading guilt feelings. Freud analyzes humor in great
detail in *Jokes and Their Relation to the Unconscious,* one of his most
impressive works. Freud was drawn to the study of humor—a subject
that has never been satisfactorily explained—because of his interest in
the psyche, the unconscious, and human aggressiveness.

JUNGIAN PSYCHOANALYTIC THEORY

Carl Jung is, after Freud, probably the most important psychoanalytic theorist. He was originally associated with Freud, but he moved away from Freud's ideas and founded his own school of "analytic psychology." Jung elaborated a number of concepts that have led to different ways of helping people and, for our purposes, of analyzing texts. Some of these concepts are discussed briefly below.

Archetype

An archetype is a universal theme found, according to Jung, in dreams, myths, religions, and works of art. Archetypes exist independent of the personal unconscious of individuals. They are connected, Jung theorized, to past history and an alleged collective unconscious found in all people. Archetypes are unconscious, Jungians argue, and we become aware of them only as the result of images that come to us in dreams, works of art, or everyday emotional experiences we have that connect us to them in ways that, suddenly, we recognize. As Jung (1964) explains:

> What we properly call instincts are physiological urges, and are perceived by the senses. But at the same time, they also manifest themselves in fantasies and often reveal their presence only by symbolic images. These manifestations are what I call the archetypes. They are without known origin; and they reproduce themselves in any time or in any part of the world—even where transmission by direct descent or "cross fertilization" through migration must be ruled out. (p. 69)

Jung suggests that "the hero figure is an archetype, which has existed since time immemorial" (p. 73), and so the same applies to the myth of Paradise or of a past "golden age," when people lived in peace and abundance.

Collective Unconscious

The source of Jung's archetypes is what he describes as the *collective unconscious*. As Jung (1964) explains, making an analogy with instincts:

> We do not assume that each new-born animal creates its own instincts as an individual acquisition, and we must not suppose that human individuals invent their specific human ways with every new birth. Like the instincts, the collective thought patterns of the human mind are innate and inherited. They function, when the occasion arises, in more or less the same way in all of us. (p. 75)

This explains, Jungians argue, why myths are universal and certain themes and motifs are found in works of art throughout history and everywhere in the world. Jung's notions about archetypes, the collective unconscious, and the universality of myths, I should add, are very controversial and many psychologists and others take issue with them. It is impossible to demonstrate, for instance, that a collective unconscious actually exists.

The Myth of the Hero

Heroes, which are archetypes and manifestations of the collective unconscious, play an important role in Jungian thought. As one prominent Jungian, Joseph L. Henderson (1964), notes:

> The myth of the hero is the most common and the best-known myth in the world. We find it in the classical mythology of Greece and Rome, in the Middle Ages, in the Far East, and among contemporary primitive tribes. It also appears in our dreams. . . .
>
> These hero myths vary enormously in detail, but the more closely one examines them the more one sees that structurally they are very similar. They have, that is to say, a universal pattern, even though they were developed by groups or individuals without any direct cultural contact with each other. . . . Over and over again one hears a tale describing a hero's miraculous but humble birth, his early proof of superhuman strength, his rapid rise to prominence or power, his triumphant struggle with the forces of evil, his fallibility to the sin of pride (*hybris*), and his fall through betrayal or a "heroic" sacrifice that ends in his death. (p. 110)

This description applies to so-called tragic heroes. Most heroes, especially those found in the mass media, generally don't succumb to the sin of pride; they usually survive to fight, in endless succession, new villains, who keep appearing with incredible regularity. The myth of the hero, according to Henderson, has the function of helping individuals develop their ego consciousness, which enables them to deal with problems they will confront as they grow older. Heroic figures help people with problems of separation and individuation from their parents and other tutelary figures, which explains why they are found throughout history and why they are so important.

The Shadow Element in the Psyche

What Jungians call the *shadow* refers to the dark side of the human psyche, which we generally keep hidden from our consciousness, though it is something that must eventually be recognized and dealt with. Henderson (1968) explains Jung's understanding of the shadow:

> Dr. Jung has pointed out that the shadow cast by the conscious mind of the individual contains the hidden, repressed, and unfavorable (or nefarious) aspects of the personality. But this darkness is not just the simple converse of the conscious ego. Just as the ego contains unfavorable and destructive attitudes, so the shadow has good qualities—normal instincts and creative impulses. Ego and shadow, indeed, although separate, are inextricably linked together in much the same way that thought and feeling are related to each other. (p. 110)

There is, then, according to Jungians, a battle for deliverance that occurs in the psyche between the shadow and the ego. Heroes provide the means (or are the vehicles) by which, symbolically, the ego "liberates the mature man from a regressive longing to return to the blissful state of infancy in a world dominated by his mother" (Henderson, 1964, pp. 111).

Freudians do not have this concept, but it is easy to see that it is vaguely analogous to what Freudians describe as the unconscious. The struggle for dominance between the shadow and the ego may be compared with the battle that Freudians assert goes on between the id and the superego, which the ego tries to mediate. Jung's shadow seems to be more negative than Freud's id, but both are considered to be the source of creative activity.

The Anima and the Animus

In Jungian thought, the anima represents the female element found in all males and the animus represents the male element found in all females. This duality, according to Jungians, is symbolized in hermaphrodites (people with the sexual organs of both sexes) and in witches, priestesses, medicine men, and shamans. M.-L. von Franz (1964), a Jungian theorist, discusses the anima and animus in terms of their impact on personality, the arts, and related phenomena:

> The most frequent manifestation of the anima takes the form of erotic fantasy. Men may be driven to nurse their fantasies by looking at films and strip-tease shows, or by day-dreaming over pornographic material. This is a crude, primitive aspect of the anima, which becomes compulsive only when a man does not sufficiently cultivate his feeling relationships—when his feeling attitude toward life has remained infantile. (pp. 179-180)

Von Franz suggests that the anima has a positive side, however, that enables men to do such things as find the right marriage partners and explore their inner values, leading them to more profound insights into their own psyches. The animus functions in much the same way for women. It is formed, von Franz suggests, essentially by the woman's father, and can have positive and negative influences. It can lead to coldness, obstinacy, and hypercritical behavior, but, conversely, it can help a woman to develop inner strength, to take an enterprising approach to life, and to relate to men in positive ways.

PSYCHOANALYTIC ANALYSIS
OF MEDIA: A CAUTIONARY NOTE

A subject as vast and complicated as the psyche poses enormous problems for a writer who wants to suggest how psychoanalytic concepts can be applied to analysis of the mass media. As with any other subject, there is always the problem of oversimplification and reductionist thinking. In this chapter I have attempted to suggest how the most fundamental concepts in psychoanalytic literature can be applied to the media—how they may help us to understand human motivation and perhaps also our reactions to what we read, see, and hear.

Because there are so many competing schools of psychoanalytic thought, and because the general public, which is not familiar with many of the concepts used by psychoanalytic thinkers, is often hostile to these concepts, psychoanalytic criticism is a difficult pursuit. But how else can we understand the way *King Kong* or *Star Trek* or *Hamlet* (or any other work in print or film media) has the power to seize our attention and move us in profound and interesting ways?

What Simon Lesser says about literature in *Fiction and the Unconscious* (1957) can be applied to just about all media:

> The supreme virtue of psychoanalysis, from the point of view of its potential utility for literary study, is that it has investigated the very aspects of man's nature with which the greatest writers of fiction have been preoccupied: the emotional, unconscious or only partly comprehended bases of our behavior. Unlike other psychologies, but like Sophocles and Shakespeare, Tolstoy and Dostoevsky, Melville and Hawthorne, it has concerned itself with the surging, non-rational forces which play so large a part in determining our destiny as well as the part of our being which tries, often in vain, to control and direct them. It offers us a systematic and well-validated body of knowledge about those forces. (p. 15)

Lesser goes on, then, to say something about what we would call the audience and the way it responds to fiction and media in general:

> It is my assumption that as we read we unconsciously *understand* at least some of a story's secret significance; to some extent our enjoyment is a product of this understanding. But some readers go on to try to account for the effect a story has had upon them, and to report what they discover. It is in connection with these later critical activities, which must be sharply differentiated I believe from the reading experience itself, that psychoanalytic concepts are likely to prove invaluable. They make it possible to deal with a portion of our response which was not hitherto accessible to criticism—permit us to explain reactions which were intuitive, fugitive and often non-verbal, and supply the key to the elements in the story responsible for those reactions. (p. 15)

To conclude, I would like to emphasize that my purpose in this chapter has not been to provide a comprehensive review of psychoanalytic techniques, but to propose the usefulness of psychoanalytic criticism for helping us to understand and interpret both what we find carried by the mass media and our responses to it—a suggestion worth some thought.

STUDY QUESTIONS AND
TOPICS FOR DISCUSSION

1. What is meant by *the unconscious*?
2. The mental life of a human being is often compared to an iceberg. Draw this iceberg and show how it can be understood to represents mental life.
3. How did Dichter explain the use of cigarette lighters? How does this explanation relate to the psyche?
4. List and discuss the four stages of development that people pass through, according to Freud.
5. What, according to Freud, are the characteristics of anal eroticism?
6. Contrast Freud's topographic hypothesis with his structural hypothesis.
7. What is the Oedipus complex, and how has it been used to explain Shakespeare's *Hamlet*?
8. What did Freud say about symbols and how do symbols function in dreams?
9. Describe and explain condensation, displacement, and secondary elaboration.
10. List and briefly describe six of the most important defense mechanisms and tell what roles they play.
11. How does the psyche handle guilt? Where does humor come in here?
12. What do Jungians believe about archetypes, the collective unconscious, the shadow, and the anima and animus?
13. What cautions should one observe in approaching analysis of media (or anything else) from a psychoanalytic perspective?

ANNOTATED BIBLIOGRAPHY

Bettelheim, Bruno. (1977). *The uses of enchantment: The meaning and importance of fairy tales.* New York: Vintage. This is an excellent example of the application of psychoanalytic theory (Freudian, in particular) to an important literary genre. Extended and perceptive readings of some of the most important Western fairy tales appear in the second half of the book.

Brenner, Charles. (1974). *An elementary textbook of psychoanalysis.* Garden City, NY: Doubleday. This is a classic textbook on psychoanalytic theory, authoritative and relatively easy to read and understand.

Freud, Sigmund. (1963). *Character and culture* (Philip Rieff, Ed.). New York: Collier. This collection of Freud's work focuses on folklore, myth, literature, and the arts—that is, applications of his theories to cultural phenomena.

Freud, Sigmund. (1965). *The interpretation of dreams.* New York: Avon. (Original work published 1900.) This is considered Freud's greatest book—a fascinating and controversial analysis of the nature of dreams and the role they play in our lives. Freud's discussions of symbols, condensation, displacement, and distortion are of particular interest to those interested in visual communication.

Fromm, Erich. (1951). *The forgotten language: An introduction to the understanding of dreams, fairy tales and myths.* New York: Grove. Fromm provides an interesting study of myths and dreams, with an extended comparison of the ideas of Jung and Freud.

Garber, Marjorie. (1993). *Vested interests: Cross-dressing and cultural anxiety.* New York: HarperPerennial. Encyclopedic, erudite, and fascinating, this book deals with various aspects of cross-dressing as it is found in print fiction, film, television, and everyday life.

Grotjahn, Martin. (1966). *Beyond laughter: Humor and the subconscious.* New York: McGraw-Hill. This fascinating study of humor and popular culture in general covers a lot of territory and has interesting things to say about many different topics.

Grotjahn, Martin. (1971). *The voice of the symbol.* New York: Delta. This classic study of the role of symbolism in media, the arts, dreams, and psychoanalytic theory includes chapters on television, Oedipus as a symbol, medieval Christian art, and symbolism in psychoanalytic theory.

Jung, Carl G., with M.-L. von Franz, Joseph L. Henderson, Jolande Jacobi, & Aniela Jaffé. (1968). *Man and his symbols.* Garden City, NY: Doubleday. This book, conceived and edited by Jung, contains chapters by Jung and some of his followers on myths, dreams, heroic types, and other Jungian concerns. Many illustrations are provided.

Key, Wilson Bryan. (1974). *Subliminal seduction: Ad media's manipulation of a not so innocent America.* New York: Signet. This remarkable (some would say notorious) volume offers all kinds of notions about the role of subliminal communication in advertising. Key's thesis is that advertisers manipulate people by sending messages that have impacts below the level of consciousness. The book includes an introduction by Marshall McLuhan.

Kolbenschlag, Madonna. (1980). *Kiss Sleeping Beauty goodbye: Breaking the spell of feminine myths and models.* Garden City, NY: Doubleday. This book argues that some women identify too strongly with the heroines in fairy tales and thus fail to develop themselves as persons. Many wait, like Sleeping Beauty, for the perfect man to come and rescue them from lives that are boring and uneventful.

Kris, Ernst. (1964). *Psychoanalytic explorations in art.* New York: Schocken. This is an important book on the creative process, literary criticism, the comic, and art.

Lesser, Simon O. (1957). *Fiction and the unconscious.* Boston: Beacon. This psychoanalytic study of fiction is useful for those interested in popular culture and the public arts.

Phillips, William. (Ed.). (1963). *Art and psychoanalysis: Studies in the application of psychoanalytic theory to the creative process.* New York: Meridian. This is a collection of essays on art, literature, and the creative process, psychological criticism, and related matters.

Rank, Otto. (1979). *The double: A psychoanalytic study.* New York: Meridian. Otto provides a fascinating study of the double motif (doppelgänger) as it is found in myths and literary and artistic texts.

Spector, Jack J. (1974). *The aesthetics of Freud: A study in psychoanalysis and art.* New York: McGraw-Hill. This is a study of Freud's theories of art and his influence on art and literature, with attention paid to biographical matters.

Winick, Charles. (1995). *Desexualization in American life.* New Brunswick, NJ: Transaction. In this provocative and controversial book, Winick argues that in the past 30 years a remarkable process of desexualization has taken place in U.S. society that is reflected in fashion, sports, the media, and popular culture. He asserts, in essence, that symbolically men are becoming weaker and women stronger.

Much of the debate about media in contemporary society has a sociological dimension, so this chapter addresses, first, the sociological concepts that have the most immediate applicability to media analysis. This is followed by a discussion of uses and gratifications theory, which includes a list of some of the reasons people use the mass media—that is, the uses and gratifications connected to the media. The chapter ends with a discussion of content analysis and a simple content analysis exercise that may yield interesting results.

CHAPTER 4

Sociological Analysis

S omeone once defined a sociologist as a person "who tells everyone things they already know in language they can't understand." I use the term *sociological* in this chapter in the broadest sense possible. The focus here will be on the social relationships of men and women, in contrast, for example, to psychological matters such as the consciousness of individuals. We will examine the public arts with a concern for human interactions and personal relationships, asking, Who does what to whom and why? and What patterns are discernible in the material we study?

It is useful to differentiate sociology from other social sciences, such as anthropology, political science, and psychology, by looking at the core concepts of these differing fields. The basic concern in sociology is how groups and institutions function (*institutions* are generally understood to be ways of patterning and organizing social life). The core concepts in psychology, as I have mentioned previously, are the individual psyche and the unconscious. For anthropologists, the core concept is culture; for political scientists, the core concepts are power and government. Different disciplines are also often combined, so we have social psychologists, political sociologists, social anthropologists, and so on.

Table 4.1 shows (in highly simplified form) the core concepts found in four of the social sciences and the terms used by social scientists in these areas for the processes through which individuals are turned into members of society. These processes don't always take place in all

TABLE 4.1 Core Concepts and Processes in Four of the Social Sciences

	Sociology	Psychology	Political Science	Anthropology
Core concept	groups, institutions	psyche, consciousness	power, government	culture
Process	socialization	identification	indoctrination	enculturation

individuals, thus we speak of people who are improperly socialized or who, because they have not been enculturated into a given culture (travelers or aliens, for example), experience "culture shock."

The term *sociology* was coined by French philosopher Auguste Comte (1798-1857), who conceived of it as a means of integrating theoretical and practical knowledge about human beings. The purpose of sociology is, according to Comte, "to know in order to predict in order to control." Comte wanted to discover the laws by which people live, so that a rational and humane social order could be established. Since Comte's time, sociology has evolved, and we find sociologists studying everything from collective behavior, deviance, and religion to the ways bureaucracies function and how social change occurs.

In this chapter, I will first discuss some of the basic concepts and tools of analysis that sociologists use when they study societies. These concepts and tools can enable us to see things we might have neglected previously. For example, take the concept of roles. Only in recent years have media critics paid much attention to the roles given to women in films and television programs, as well as to such related matters as the numbers of women relative to the numbers of men, the ages of the women portrayed, and what happens to them. An understanding of some important sociological concepts can help an analyst to examine the mass media in new ways.

Following the discussion of basic concepts, I will address the gratifications the public arts offer to people and the needs that people use the mass media to meet. In recent years there has been a good deal of interest in this *uses and gratifications* approach (sometimes also called the *needs and gratifications* approach). The focus here will be on how people use the media and the gratifications the media offer them. I will suggest a number of needs and gratifications that are met by the public arts; this list may shed some light on why certain television programs, films, and other media products are so popular, as well as the roles they might play in society.

The chapter ends with a discussion of a standard sociological technique, content analysis. In conducting content analysis, researchers use statistical methods to make inferences about what they find in the media. Take the matter of violence on children's television programs as an example. Once we decide upon a working definition of *violence,* we can examine a sampling of children's television programs and count the incidents of violence we find. This enables us to move from saying, "There's a lot of violence on children's television," to something like, "There are X incidents of violence per hour on children's television."

Frequently, researchers using content analysis adopt a historical frame of reference. They might examine, for instance, earlier samples of children's programs in order to make comparisons concerning the violence they contain. Using content analysis techniques, researchers can determine whether there is more violence in children's television programs now than there was at some earlier time. If there is more violence now, what does that mean?

SOME BASIC CONCEPTS

Following are brief discussions of some fundamental sociological concepts, all of which can be applied to analysis of the public arts. The explanations are as concise as I can make them; I hope that in my effort to be clear I have not oversimplified matters too greatly.

Alienation

Alienation means, literally, "no ties," and refers to a feeling of estrangement and separation from others. A person who is alienated feels like "a stranger" (alien), with no connections to his or her society or to some group in that society. Feelings of alienation are connected, in many instances, to the bureaucracies that develop in organizations. Bureaucracies are often necessary to deal with large numbers of people in a fair and efficient manner, but they are also impersonal and tend to generate feelings of alienation. Students in large universities are frequently known to the administration only by their social security numbers, and our language about students also has an alienating tone. We sometimes talk about young men and women as being "college material," for instance.

We can use the concept of alienation to understand the behavior of characters in texts—such as Willy Loman in *Death of a Salesman*—and of social groups and subcultures—teenagers, punk rockers, and so on. When we apply this concept we must connect it, very specifically, to acts of characters or the behaviors of groups and subcultures.

Anomie

The word *anomie* is derived from the Greek word *nomos,* meaning "norms." A person who rejects the norms of a given society is described as anomic. Anomie and alienation are quite different. A group of thieves, for example, might have a strong sense of fellowship and thus not be alienated, but because they have no respect for the laws of society, they would be described as anomic.

Bureaucracy

As society becomes larger and more complex, it becomes increasingly difficult to regulate, and keeping things running with any degree of efficiency can be a problem. Bureaucracies are collections of more or less anonymous people who follow fixed rules and routines in running organizations. There is usually a hierarchy of authority, impersonal handling of problems, and a great deal of red tape.

Class (Socioeconomic)

A class is a group of people with something in common. When used in a sociological context, the term usually refers to socioeconomic class—a person's class level or place in the hierarchy of classes that exists in society. W. Lloyd Warner (1953), a distinguished sociologist and anthropologist, has suggested that there are six classes in American society: upper-upper, lower-upper, upper-middle, lower-middle, upper-lower, and lower-lower. Warner's estimates of the distribution of membership in these classes in the population of the United States are as follows:

upper-upper, 1.4%
lower-upper, 1.6%
upper-middle, 10%
lower-middle, 28%
upper-lower, 33%
lower-lower, 25%

Warner suggests that the lower-middle and upper-lower classes constitute the "common man" level. These figures are dated, but they give an idea of the class makeup of U.S. society that is still fairly accurate.

Socioeconomic class is determined by a number of components, including education, income, and occupation, and different social classes have different lifestyles, ways of raising children, and values.

As of the early 1980s, it was estimated that the wealthiest 1% of American families owned more than 40% of all the corporate stock in the country, and the top 10% controlled almost 70% of the total wealth. This 10% owned around half the value of all real estate and more than 90% of business corporate stocks and business assets and bonds. There were approximately 80 million families in the United States at that time, but 400,000 households controlled 27% of the wealth. Since these figures were compiled, the concentration of wealth has increased. The lowest 25% of American families have been losing ground, economically.

Thus, although many Americans tend to think of the United States as an essentially "classless," "all-middle-class" society, it is actually very much a class-based society. There is a substantial middle class, but there is very definitely an economic elite in the United States that has enormous political power.

Deviance

Deviance refers to behavioral patterns that are different from typical or conventional (some would say normal) ones. Attitudes toward different forms of deviance change over time. For instance, homosexuality was once considered criminal but now is defined as deviant and is tolerated by most people. Deviance generates anxiety among people because it forces them to consider how valid their own practices are as well as the correctness of their own attitudes about what is normal.

Elites

Elites are the people at the top of the social pyramid, the upper-class and lower-upper-class people who hold positions of power, who are affluent, and who generally work in professional or executive occupations. (The opposite of elites would be common men and women.) It has been documented that the heroes on television tend to be relatively young, well-educated, White professionals; the entertainment media present very few working-class heroes. We might wonder what effects this overrepresentation of elites has on the viewing audience.

Ethnicity

Ethnicity is conventionally understood to mean certain cultural traits and traditions that distinguish various groups existing in a society. Thus Italians, Poles, Germans, Finns, Jews (who are a special case), and countless other groups are all considered to be ethnics. In the past, some members of particular ethnic groups tried to camouflage their identities in the United States, but today it is common for people to be proud of their heritages. Ethnic groups are often stereotyped in the media, though this practice is now under attack.

Functionalism

Sociologists say that something is *functional* when it contributes to the maintenance and stability of whatever entity it is part of; likewise, something is *dysfunctional* if it is a destabilizing or destructive factor. If something has no particular effect on the entity it is part of, it is said to be *nonfunctional*. What complicates matters is that something may be functional in some regards and dysfunctional in others at the same time. Thus television in general may be functional in that it provides a great deal of information to people, helps fuel consumption, and stresses certain values, but it may be dysfunctional in that it portrays many people in negative roles, suggests that the world is more violent than it really is, and creates feelings of anxiety and discontent in people who cannot afford all of the good (and bad) things advertised on television. There is a conservative bias to functional analysis in that it emphasizes the maintenance and stability of society, instead of focusing on changes that might be made.

We can also examine phenomena in terms of whether their functions are intended or unintended, conscious or unconscious. Thus the *manifest function* of news programs might be to inform people, whereas the *latent function* of these programs might be to indoctrinate people with certain political values and beliefs. The reporters and newscasters, I should point out, may not be aware that they are indoctrinating people; they may believe that all they are doing is reporting the news.

Media analysts are interested in the roles that individual performers play in texts and in the roles assigned to women, to members of ethnic and racial minorities, to old and young people, and to representatives of other groups (sexual, political, religious, socioeconomic) as well. Viewers of films and television programs often identify with the heroes and heroines in these texts and incorporate what they see in creating their own identities. Many believe that a considerable amount of "social teaching" is generated by the mass media.

Many critics argue that the roles that women play in the media are often demeaning. Women are all too frequently treated only as sexual objects, used for display, or portrayed as dummies who get excited about some brand of toilet paper. They are much less often shown as professionals or other productive citizens who should be taken seriously. Frequently, they appear only as passive figures who react to the initiatives of others, usually males. Such roles give audience members images of what women are like and how they should be treated that can have negative consequences not only for women, but for men as well. I could also discuss the negative ways Blacks, Asians, Latinos, Jews, disabled persons, and countless other groups are portrayed in the media.

When media analysts look at roles in the media from a sociological perspective, then, they must examine the roles assigned to people (who must be seen as representatives of social groups) and the impacts that media dissemination of these roles might have upon individuals and society in general.

Another concept of interest in the area of functionalism is that of *functional alternatives*. Sociologists use this idea to explain situations in which, for example, an original institution loses its viability (to some extent) and is replaced by a substitute institution. According to functionalist theory, institutions are created and evolve because certain things have to be done to keep a society operating properly. If a given institution no longer works, something must be found to take its place. Let us assume, for example, that people have a need for some kind of religious experience, some form of connection with powers beyond the human. This need, in the United States, has traditionally been taken care of by organized religions. But as mainline organized religions have lost popularity, something else has been needed to take their place, and professional football has to a degree filled that function. Professional football might be seen, from this perspective, as a functional alternative to organized religion. (This idea is discussed in more detail in Chapter 6.)

All the different aspects of functional analysis may be summarized as follows:

- ✔ *functional:* maintains an organization, society, or the like
- ✔ *dysfunctional:* destabilizes an organization, society, or the like
- ✔ *nonfunctional:* plays no role
- ✔ *manifest function:* intended and recognized by people
- ✔ *latent function:* not intended and not recognized by people
- ✔ *functional alternative:* substitutes for original institution, practice

Lifestyle

Lifestyle is a comprehensive term that covers a person's tastes in fashion, cars, entertainment and recreation, literature, and related matters. *Style* suggests fashion, and *lifestyle* is used to describe how a person fashions his or her life. Lifestyle is often connected to socioeconomic class, and is reflected in a person's "image."

People's lifestyles are reflected in their various taste decisions: the kinds of cars they drive, the breeds of dogs or cats they own, the magazines they read (or at least display on the coffee table), where they live, what their homes are like (how big, the color of the walls, the kind of furniture), their occupations, the kinds of food they eat and the restaurants they frequent, the kinds of vacations they take—the list is endless. All of these phenomena tend to be class specific and are reflections of an individual's class and so-called level of sophistication. The institution that tutors us about these matters is advertising, one of whose basic functions is to make sure, to the extent it can, that "expenditure always rises to meet, if not exceed, income."

Marginalization

Marginalization is the process by which individuals and groups with (in some cases deviant) values and beliefs that differ from the norm in societies are delegitimated and given secondary status. This may involve being ignored or persecuted or both. As the United States becomes a more diverse and segmented multicultural society, with numerous linguistic, racial, sexual, and other subcultures, there is some question as to whether dominant elites and majority members will continue to be able to marginalize members of "out-groups" and subcultures with different demographic descriptions.

Mass Communication and Mass Media

Sociologists and communication scholars distinguish between mass communication and the mass media. We live in an age in which mass communication is held to be of major importance in our lives. Mass communication involves the use of the mass media—print media such as newspapers and magazines and electronic media such as radio, television, and films (and now the Internet)—to communicate with large numbers of people at the same time. These media reach people in groups in some cases and lone individuals in other cases.

Sociologists have developed numerous models to explain how mass communication works. These models are highly abstract representations of the process of communication, the role of media in communication, and related concerns. One of the most famous of these is Harold Lasswell's theory, which asks, "Who? Says what? In which channel? To whom? With what effect?" (quoted in McQuail & Windahl, 1993, p. 13). There are numerous debates ongoing among communication researchers, regarding, for instance, whether the mass media are weak or powerful and what effects they have on individuals and societies.

Mass Society

A number of years ago, some sociologists argued that the United States had become what they described as a mass society—that is, a society in which large numbers of people live in given areas but have little involvement with one another, and thus are susceptible to manipulation. As Herbert Blumer, a prominent sociologist, wrote in 1936:

> [The mass] has no social organization, no body of customs and traditions, no established set of rules or rituals, no organized group of sentiments, no structure or status roles, and no established leadership. It merely consists of an aggregation of individuals who are separate, detached, anonymous. (quoted in Friedson, 1953, p. 314)

This notion of a mass society is not accepted by many social scientists and has been attacked as being based on theory and not on the ways people behave in contemporary societies.

Postmodernism

There are so many different definitions of *postmodernism* that some scholars suggest it can mean anything you want it to mean. According to some critics, postmodernism has had profound effects on American culture and society and has played a major role in shaping our consciousness. Fredric Jameson (1991), a literature professor at Duke University, has suggested that postmodernism is a "cultural dominant" that represents the latest stage of capitalism. Others take issue with this notion.

One of the best descriptions of postmodernism comes from sociologist Todd Gitlin (1989):

> It self-consciously splices genres, attitudes, styles. It relishes the blurring or juxtaposition of forms (fiction-nonfiction), stances (straight-ironic), moods (violent-comic), cultural levels (high-low). . . .
>
> One postmodernist trope is the list, as if culture were a garage sale, so it is appropriate to evoke postmodernism by offering a list of examples, for better or worse: Michael Graves' Portland Building, Philip Johnson's AT&T, and hundreds of more or less skillful derivatives; Robert Rauschenberg's silk screens; Andy Warhol's multiple-image paintings, photo-realism . . . ; Disneyland, Las Vegas, suburban

strips, shopping malls, mirror-glass office building facades; William Burroughs, Tom Wolfe, Donald Barthelme, Monty Python, Don De-Lillo, Joe Isuzu "He's Lying" commercials, Philip Glass, *Star Wars,* Spalding Gray, David Hockney, . . . Max Headroom, David Byrne, Twyla Tharpe (choreographing Beach Boys and Frank Sinatra songs), Italo Calvino. (pp. 52-53)

What this list points out is the extent to which our consciousness has been shaped by postmodernism. If the postmodernist theorists are correct, many Americans who have never even heard the term *postmodernism* (though it is showing up now increasingly in popular magazines and newspapers) are living, though they may not realize it, postmodern lives. To adopt a medical analogy, Gitlin's list reflects the symptoms; postmodernism is the disease.

Race

David Dressler (1969) defines race as "a category of people with a common genetic heritage" and notes that physical anthropologists "often cited three broad classifications of race: *Negroid, Mongoloid* and *Caucasoid* (although other divisions are sometimes listed)" (pp. 518-519). Race, it must be added, is not the same thing as ethnicity, which is connected to nationality and not genetic makeup. I mention the subject of race because historically there has been a considerable amount of racism in the public arts, and it is still a problem.

Role (Social)

We are all familiar with the term *role* as it is used in theater, television, and film; the concept of social role is in some ways similar. Social roles are formed by certain kinds of behavior that we learn, that relate to expectations people have of us, that are connected to specific situations; these roles are determined, in part, by an individual's place in society. In the course of a day, the average individual plays many roles: parent, worker, companion, and so on.

Sex (Gender)

Sex is an important sociological concept when it is linked to roles and some of the other concepts discussed here. Many media critics argue that the mass media are sexist and have consistently assigned women to destructive roles. This is certainly an important issue for media analysts to keep in mind.

Sociologist E. Barbara Phillips conducted a content analysis that is instructive in this area. She analyzed random selections from two magazines—*Ms.* and *Family Circle*—and discovered considerable differences between them. For example, the women who were the subjects of articles in *Family Circle* were all homemakers; *Family Circle* included no articles about women who were involved in politics or social concerns. The articles in *Ms.*, on the other hand, didn't deal with any women as homemakers (though many of the subjects were married and had families); rather, they focused only on the ways the women were involved in social, cultural, and political life and public service. The two magazines projected different roles for women and, no doubt, each helped to support and reinforce the value systems of its readers.

Socialization

Socialization is the process by which people are taught the rules, roles, and values of their society. It may be seen as a kind of indoctrination that is done formally through institutions, such as the family, the school system, and the church, and informally through the media. What is important about informal socialization is that people generally do not recognize that they are being taught (some would say programmed) what roles to play and how to play them, what values to espouse, what attitudes to have, what goals to strive for, and so on.

Status

Status is often confused with role, but the two are actually quite different, although connected. *Status* refers to the position a person has in some group or organization and the prestige attached to that position. Status is thus associated with a person's role. Within universities, for example, full professors have more status than assistant professors and play different roles. Within society in general those who have certain occupations have great status (doctors, lawyers, professors, bankers) and others have little status (ditch diggers). Status is a powerful force in society that is used to control people in subtle ways.

Stereotype

Horton and Hunt (1972) define a stereotype as *"a group-shared image of another group or category of people.* Stereotypes can be positive (the kindly, dedicated family doctor), negative (the unprincipled, opportunistic politician) or mixed (the dedicated, fussy, sexless, old-maid school teacher)" (p. 163). Regardless of whether stereotypes are positive or negative, they are dangerous. They give millions of people oversimplified and sometimes pernicious images of Blacks, Jews, Frenchmen, doctors, police officers, women—the list could be endless. No matter what the form—racial stereotyping, occupational stereotyping, sex role stereotyping, or some other—stereotypes are oversimplifications and overgeneralizations that minimize individual differences; they tend to be very destructive.

Values

Values are the attitudes that people have relative to what they believe to be desirable and undesirable, good and bad; they cover a wide spectrum of social phenomena, including sex, politics, and education. In indirect ways, people's values affect their behaviors. Media critics must be aware of the values of the characters portrayed in mass-mediated productions and should examine what these values suggest about society.

The preceding minicourse in sociological concepts is meant to alert you to some of the concerns sociologists (and other social scientists) have, and what they look at when they examine the public arts. As I have pointed out, frequently it is useful to combine concepts, so we might consider such matters as sex role stereotyping, socioeconomic class and status, racism and sexism (and all the other *isms*), and the values of deviants. Readers who are interested in exploring these concepts in more detail and within the structure of sociological theory in general should consult any of the standard introductory sociology texts; also, the annotated bibliography at the end of this chapter lists some important books that take a "media sociology" approach.

I should note here that media analysts need to bear in mind that they are concerned with works of art when they examine sitcoms, soap operas, commercials, and all the other genres found in the public arts. These texts cannot be considered merely documents to be viewed in terms of their sociological content; other considerations must be taken into account, such as artistic conventions and the difficulties involved in dealing with some artistic or creative personalities.

USES AND GRATIFICATIONS

There is a good deal of controversy related to uses and gratifications theory, but the same can be said about every other theory related to media. Despite the fact that much of the research so far conducted on the mass media has been of an empirical nature and has been concerned with the effects media have on attitudes (and many other matters), there has been a considerable amount of interest in the ways people use media and the gratifications media offer to people. Katz, Blumler, and Gurevitch (1979) mention some early works on the subject:

> Herzog (1942) on quiz programs and the gratifications derived from listening to soap operas; Suchman (1942) on the motives for getting interested in serious music on radio; Wolfe and Fiske (1949) on the development of children's interest in comics; Berelson (1949) on the functions of newspaper reading; and so on. Each of these investigations came up with a list of functions served either by some specific contents or by the medium in question: to match one's wits against others, to get information or advice for daily living, to provide a framework for one's day, to prepare oneself culturally for the demands of upward mobility, or to be reassured about the dignity and usefulness of one's role. (p. 215)

Regardless of whether you think that soap operas are stupid or that situation comedies are silly, the functions these programs—and others—perform for people may in some cases be quite important.

Below, I list and briefly describe a number of suggested gratifications that the media offer and some needs they may help to fill. A good deal of scientific work remains to be done on people's needs, on the gratifications individuals seek, and on the roles the mass media play in meeting people's needs, but it seems obvious that people do use media (though they may not be aware they are doing so) in varying ways.

The material that follows comes from a number of different sources, but I am particularly indebted to my colleague Stuart Hyde, who has addressed in his work a number of the needs and desires people have and the ways they use the public arts to deal with them. It is difficult to decide, in some cases, whether a given reason people use the media involves needs, uses, gratifications, or desires, so in the following list of reasons I avoid these terms altogether, leaving those issues for you to determine. The list is also incomplete; you may be able to add to it in ways that will help you to understand more fully how the media function.

To be amused. We seem to want to be entertained, to find things to laugh about, to be put in a happy spirit. The media are a source of positive pleasure.

To see authority figures exalted or deflated. American society has its roots in egalitarian values, and many Americans tend to regard authority as invalid. Thus we like to see authority figures deflated and ridiculed, especially politicians, soldiers, professors, and psychiatrists. There are some authority figures we tend to exalt, however: clergymen, surgeons, and detectives, to name a few. The media play an important role in teaching us how to relate to authority and to deal with authority figures.

To experience the beautiful. We give high status to beautiful music, beautiful works of art, and people who are physically attractive—in particular, beautiful women. What is beautiful is another matter, however, and definitions of beauty change over time.

To share experiences with others (community). One of the more important functions of the mass media is to give people a common cultural (or pop cultural) frame of reference. In some cases, such as when we go to football games in huge stadiums, we are actually with others in a momentary kind of community. And this experience is often shared with millions of others who may listen to the game on the radio or watch it on television. In other cases we merely watch a program "along with" millions of others. It has been discovered that one of the most important topics of conversation among Americans is the content of the media; thus sharing the same programs or films may help people relate to one another.

To satisfy curiosity and to be informed. This has to do with our wish to know what's going on, to be up-to-date, to follow stories as they develop, and so on. The satisfaction of curiosity probably has to do with human beings' natural inquisitiveness, whereas the desire to know what's going on and to be informed has to do with surveillance and the anxiety we feel when we are "in the dark." One thing is certain—we learn a great deal from the media, both directly and indirectly.

To identify with the deity and the divine plan. Many people have some form of what might be called "the God concept," and the media often help people gain a sense of the nature of life, the power of spiritual forces, and so forth.

To find distraction and diversion. Many people find that the public arts help them escape (if only momentarily) from worry and anxiety and help them pass the time when they are bored. This kind of thing is sometimes described as killing time by those who feel the public arts tend to be mindless and destructive, but from a uses and gratifications perspective, the public arts are never used only to kill time. We may *seem* to be doing nothing (and even think we are doing nothing) when we watch television or listen to rock music, but in truth a great deal is going on.

To experience empathy. We share in the joys and sorrows of others through the media and from this we derive psychological pleasure— often catharsis or "relief." Although we relate to the various characters we see in the media vicariously, we still are able to share in their emotional experiences, and this enriches us greatly. It also helps us prepare ourselves emotionally for the difficulties we all face in real life at one time or another.

To experience, in a guilt-free and controlled situation, extreme emotions, such as love and hate, the horrible and the terrible, and similar phenomena. This is slightly different from experiencing empathy, which involves identifying with characters. This concerns our desire to experience powerful emotions without being carried away by them or having to feel guilt about them. The media enable us to have powerful experiences without paying for them, so to speak, and to take risks without having to worry about being devastated. (There is some question, however, as to whether all individuals do escape being affected by their media experiences. Despite the "controls," some people may end up with morbid residues, thoughts that may trigger violence, or other effects that they are unaware of.)

To find models to imitate. These models help us to gain a sense of identity, teach us how to cope in certain situations, and, informally, socialize us. One problem here is that some people may identify with villains rather than heroes and heroines and may pick up ideas, attitudes, and behavior patterns that are harmful and destructive. For example, there is a great deal of fear that children who watch programs full of violence will learn to be violent and to use violence as a means of solving problems.

To gain identity. Identity can be defined as a coherent sense of self, a personal style, a "defined" personality. The United States is no longer a traditional society, and as our traditions wither, as we become more mobile, modern, and materialistic, we find it increasingly more difficult to form identities. This is where the media come in—and, in particular, the various heroic and unheroic figures we follow in the comics, watch on television, read about in popular novels, and so on. They help us manufacture identities, so to speak. But whether or not these identities are suitable, long lasting, and good for us is another matter.

To gain information about the world. In some cases this is obvious: In the media we hear economists talk about economic problems, professors and other experts are called upon to explain things to us, documentaries deal with topics of interest, and televised college courses are offered on some stations. But we also learn a great deal "incidentally" from the media all the time, such as how to behave in certain situations; the media offer us heroic figures to emulate, and they reinforce certain values. The media are always teaching us something, even when they are not intentionally doing so, and even when we don't realize they are doing so. A good question we might keep in mind, then, is, What are we learning from the media?

To reinforce belief in justice. It doesn't always work out this way, but generally speaking we like to see heroes defeat villains and to see evil punished and virtue rewarded. In other words, we want to believe that the universe is moral and that crime doesn't pay.

To reinforce belief in romantic love. Although our belief in the power of love may be waning, we still tend to see romantic love as a wonderful thing and as a prime motivating force in relationships. Implicit in the belief in romantic love is the notion that emotions are powerful forces that are capable, at times, of overwhelming logic, reason, class differences, age differences, racial differences, and anything else. We learn sometimes, however, that romantic love doesn't always lead to happiness.

To reinforce belief in magic, the marvelous, and the miraculous. This belief, which probably stems in great measure from childhood (fairy tales, seeing magicians, and so on), explains our interest in horror stories, science fiction, and the like. It also represents a way of dealing with the demonic.

To see others make mistakes. To err is human, it has been said. We all make mistakes, and when we see others make the same or similar mistakes we feel less guilty or upset about our own, because we can conclude that our errors are perfectly natural. In certain instances we also gain a sense of superiority, because we haven't been "stupid" enough to make *those* mistakes. In addition, we can also learn by watching others make mistakes and pay for them—mistakes that we can try to avoid.

To see order imposed on the world. We want to believe that the universe makes sense, that there are reasons for things being the way they are, and that we can plan ahead. The media constantly help us gain a sense of the orderliness of the world by teaching us about such things as the laws of nature, human psychology and motivation, and social phenomena.

To participate vicariously in history. We all want to be on the scene when important events take place—to be there when the big ball games are played, to hear what politicians have to say when history is being made—and the media help us do this. We can even spend our evenings overhearing (so to speak) celebrities chatting about their love lives. I would argue that this desire to "participate" in history is a powerful force in our lives and reflects our feelings of alienation and insignificance. Television allows the nobodies, huddled in front of their sets, to watch the somebodies on the talk shows.

To be purged of unpleasant emotions. The media often provide for catharsis, or purging of emotions, through art. We can discharge anger, anxiety, hostility, and a host of other negative feelings by watching plays, football games, or movies, listening to music, and so on. Some public art forms, such as soap operas and professional wrestling, provide clearly defined "hate" figures to help viewers with this purgation.

To obtain outlets for sexual drives in a guilt-free context. In recent years a number of people and groups have attacked the allegedly excessive amount of violence on television. This has led television (and other media as well) to try to find other ways of attracting and maintaining audience interest. One of these ways is humor and the other is sex. Sexuality is treated much more explicitly in films than on television, where everything tends to be implied, but where "wiggle and jiggle" or "tits and ass" now are major elements in programming. Our sexual experiences are always vicarious ones when it comes to media. Whether these vicarious experiences provide relief or generate anxiety and negative feelings (because, for example, our wives or girlfriends are not beauty queens and sex goddesses) is a matter for conjecture.

To explore taboo subjects with impunity and without risk. Because the news and entertainment media allow us to examine taboo subjects "from a distance," we are able to obtain double benefits. We can explore certain subjects and derive whatever excitement or titillation they may generate, and we can gain a sense of moral satisfaction by condemning particular practices or coming to some kind of conclusions about them. When the media examine, either dramatically or in documentary style, topics such as incest, spousal abuse, rape, drug abuse, and child beating, we get the "thrill" of finding out about these crimes and the reward of being able to condemn those involved.

To experience the ugly. This is the opposite side of our desire to experience the beautiful. People have always been fascinated with ugliness, grotesques, and monsters in rather complex ways. We are both attracted and repelled by ugliness. I should also point out that our attitudes toward what is beautiful and what is ugly are complicated by the fact that they are constantly changing.

To affirm moral, spiritual, and cultural values. Values, as noted above, are beliefs we have (which we learn from our families, friends, religions, and other institutions) about what is good and bad, desirable and undesirable, just and unjust. Our actions and conduct are based on our values, which we tend to view as "ultimate." That is, they are the bedrock upon which we build our lives and societies. Two of the most important values in American society are egalitarianism and achievement. We may not always put these values into practice, but they are goals toward which we work. The media tend to reinforce certain values and neglect others. Media analysts must be mindful of the values they find and consider whether these are positive or negative, why they are being championed, and what they reveal about the social order.

To see villains in action. Villains are often more interesting than heroes and heroines, who must be good, moral, and thoughtful—at least most of the time. (In recent years, this matter has become less simple; we often find "good-bad" heroes and "bad-good" villains.) Villains can do all kinds of things, have much more room to maneuver than do heroes, and can be of all sorts and natures. We like to see all the terrible things that villains are capable of doing, but we also like to see them punished. This gives us two satisfactions for the price of one.

To summarize, I have discussed above the following reasons people use the mass media:

1. to be amused
2. to see authority figures exalted or deflated
3. to experience the beautiful
4. to share experiences with others
5. to satisfy curiosity and be informed
6. to identify with the deity and the divine plan
7. to find distraction and diversion
8. to experience empathy
9. to experience, in a guilt-free situation, extreme emotions
10. to find models to imitate
11. to gain identity
12. to gain information about the world
13. to reinforce belief in justice
14. to reinforce belief in romantic love
15. to reinforce belief in magic, the marvelous, and the miraculous
16. to see others make mistakes
17. to see order imposed on the world
18. to participate vicariously in history
19. to be purged of unpleasant emotions
20. to obtain outlets for sexual drives in a guilt-free context
21. to explore taboo subjects with impunity
22. to experience the ugly
23. to affirm moral, spiritual, and cultural values
24. to see villains in action

When you examine a text from a uses and gratifications point of view, you must try to determine which uses and gratifications are most important and which are secondary. Also, you should be able to cite an event in the text (the film, situation comedy, soap opera, comic book, or whatever) for each use or gratification that you assert is being taken care of.

One problem with the uses and gratifications approach is that different critics often see a particular event (in a film, for instance) as being used in different ways or as providing different gratifications. This is because the uses to which people put the media are somewhat ambiguous. The uses and gratifications approach, however, helps us to understand the power the mass media have. One question that analysts must continually keep in mind when they think about the public arts is, They do a great deal *for* us, but what are they doing *to* us?

CONTENT ANALYSIS

Content analysis is a research technique that involves measuring something (counting instances of violence; determining percentages of Blacks, women, professional types, or whatever) in a random sampling of some form of communication (such as comics, sitcoms, soap operas, news shows). The basic assumption implicit in content analysis is that an investigation of messages and communication will allow some insight into the people who receive these messages.

A description of an early content analysis conducted using magazine stories may be instructive. Sociologist Leo Lowenthal (1944) studied biographies of popular heroes found in two magazines: *Collier's* and the *Saturday Evening Post.* He classified the biographies in terms of whether they dealt with political life, business and the professions, or entertainment. Lowenthal discovered several interesting things. First, there was an increase in the number of biographies over the years. Second, the number of articles on politicians and business/professionals declined and the number of articles on entertainers increased. And third, the articles on entertainers shifted from being about serious artists and writers to being about popular entertainers of one sort or another.

Lowenthal found that the earlier biographical articles focused on "idols of production" (providing education and orientation) and the later articles focused on "idols of consumption," such as movie stars and other entertainment figures. They dealt with what we would describe now as the lifestyle preferences and consumption patterns of these figures. Lowenthal discusses how these "idols of consumption" relate to such matters as attitudes toward childhood, success, adjustment, and the socializing function of these biographies. His 40-page article is frequently cited by sociologists.

Some of the advantages of content analysis are as follows:

✔ It is inexpensive.

✔ It is usually relatively easy to get material.
✔ It is unobtrusive (and thus doesn't influence people).
✔ It yields data that can be quantified.
✔ It can be used to examine current events, past events, or both.

The problems associated with content analysis include the following:

✔ It is hard to be certain that the sample studied is representative.
✔ It is often hard to obtain a good working definition of the topic being studied (for example, what is violence?).
✔ It isn't always easy to find a measurable unit, such as a frame in a comic strip. What does one do about films or magazine articles?
✔ It isn't possible to prove that the inferences made on the basis of a content analysis are correct.

Despite these problems, content analysis can often be used to conduct interesting and useful experiments. Analysts who are just beginning to use this method will find it best to choose a medium that is relatively easy to deal with. That is why the following exercise involves the analysis of comic strips. Comics offer the content analyst a number of advantages: Most people are familiar with them, the characters are easily classifiable, and the strips are easy to obtain and simple to work with. Unlike texts found in the electronic media, which flit by rapidly, comics stay stuck to the page, and an analyst can spend as much time examining them as he or she likes.

You should choose your categories for analysis based on what you want to discover. Let me suggest some possible topics:

physical characteristics of heroes and heroines, villains and villainesses

✔ color of hair
✔ color of eyes
✔ height
✔ weight
✔ age
✔ body structure
✔ sex
✔ race

social characteristics of characters

- ✔ occupation
- ✔ education
- ✔ religion
- ✔ socioeconomic class
- ✔ status
- ✔ role
- ✔ ethnic background (nationality)

emotional nature of characters

- ✔ warm or cold
- ✔ anxious or calm
- ✔ stable or unstable
- ✔ authoritarian or dependent
- ✔ hostile or friendly
- ✔ powerful or weak
- ✔ loving or hateful
- ✔ individualist or conformist
- ✔ vivacious or apathetic

These are just some of the things you might concern yourself with in a content analysis of the comics that focuses on the characters in these stories. You should also keep in mind thematic issues, such as the amount of violence (and its use), the values of the characters, allusions to social and political events, and reflections of cultural matters.

There is one other aspect of content analysis that I should mention here: Content analyses are most useful when they include a historic or comparative dimension. Although it is interesting to know, for example, how much violence there is in the daily newspaper's comics pages, it is even more interesting to know how much violence there was in that newspaper's comics pages 10 years ago, 20 years ago, 30 years ago, and so on. By taking a historical point of view, an analyst can discern trends and determine whether there have been significant changes in attitudes about (or stereotypes of) women, Blacks, ethnic groups, or any of the other topics listed above. By taking a comparative point of view, media analysts can discover how one culture's or society's values and beliefs differ from those of others.

An interesting exercise in content analysis would be to choose a comics page from some newspaper (making sure that back editions of the same paper are available on microfilm) and examine it in terms of the topics listed above as well as in terms of the average number of characters per frame, the percentages of male and female characters on the page, the numbers of words spoken by male and female characters, and the number of acts of violence. Make a comparison between what you find on the present-day page of comics and what you find on the comics page of the same paper 20, 30, or 40 years ago.

With this discussion of content analysis I bring to a conclusion my introduction to sociological perspectives on the media. It is, at best, a start, but it should provide you with a sense of the kinds of things sociologists look for when they examine media and the public arts. There is a degree of overlap with Marxist analysis here that might be expected, given that Marxist concepts inform a good deal of sociological thought. The uses and gratifications approach also has psychological dimensions.

STUDY QUESTIONS AND
TOPICS FOR DISCUSSION

1. Explain the following basic sociological concepts: bureaucracy, role, alienation, anomie, class, functionalism, marginalization, mass communication, mass media, postmodernism, sex (gender), socialization, status, stereotypes.
2. What is meant by *uses and gratifications*?
3. Do you think people today use the mass media differently compared with how people used media 10 or 20 years ago? Whatever your position, justify it.
4. What are the advantages and disadvantages of content analysis?
5. List and briefly describe any six uses and gratifications connected with the media discussed in this chapter and apply them to some well-known film or other text.

ANNOTATED BIBLIOGRAPHY

Arens, W., & Montague, Susan P. (1976). *The American dimension: Cultural myths and social realities.* New York: Alfred. This collection of articles on food, films, football, fast foods, soap operas, and more is written from an anthropological perspective.

Berger, Arthur Asa. (1976). *The TV-guided American.* New York: Walker. This book analyzes a number of television shows (*All in the Family, Kung Fu, Mission Impossible,* and more) in terms of what they reflect about U.S. culture and society.

Berger, Arthur Asa. (Ed.). (1987). *Television in society.* New Brunswick, NJ: Transaction. This is a collection of essays originally published in *Society* magazine on television shows, media events, and various social aspects of television.

Berger, Arthur Asa. (1995). *Essentials of mass communication theory.* Thousand Oaks, CA: Sage. This book offers an overview of mass communication theory, using focal points to discuss works of art, artists, audiences, society, and media and the ways these relate to one another.

Berger, Arthur Asa. (1997). *Postmortem for a postmodernist.* Walnut Creek, CA: AltaMira. This is a comic murder mystery with an international cast of zany characters that explains the basic principles of postmodernism while spoofing the mystery genre and satirizing academia. Illustrated with numerous comic-strip-framelike drawings by the author.

Berger, Arthur Asa. (1998). *Media research techniques* (2nd ed.). Thousand Oaks, CA: Sage. This book describes and assists readers in carrying out a number of research projects involving the media; it includes discussion of content analysis, focus groups, and the rhetorical analysis of magazine advertisements.

Berger, Arthur Asa. (Ed.). (1998). *The postmodern presence: Readings on postmodernism in American culture and society.* Walnut Creek, CA: AltaMira. This is a collection of essays, many never before published, that deal with the impacts of postmodernism on contemporary American culture and society. Topics addressed include MTV, film, fashion, *The X Files, The Terminator, Wayne's World,* museums, and architecture.

Berger, Peter L., & Berger, Brigitte. (1972). *Sociology: A biographical approach.* New York: Basic Books. This innovative textbook in sociology focuses on the great thinkers of the discipline and their basic ideas.

Burns, Elizabeth, & Burns, Tom. (Eds.). (1973). *Sociology of literature and drama.* New York: Penguin. This is a collection of essays by some of the most important thinkers of the contemporary period. The essays are written from a sociological point of view, though Marxist and structuralist thinkers are also included.

Jones, Steven G. (Ed.). (1997). *CyberSociety: Computer-mediated communication and community.* Thousand Oaks, CA: Sage. Everything from virtual reality and virtual worlds to Nintendo, computer games, and standards of conduct on the Internet is covered in this stimulating collection of essays.

McLuhan, Marshall. (1967). *The mechanical bride: Folklore of industrial man.* Boston: Beacon. McLuhan offers a brilliant study of the sociological significance of American advertisements and comics. This pioneering effort is still worth careful attention.

Real, Michael R. (1977). *Mass-mediated culture.* Englewood Cliffs, NJ: Prentice Hall. Real provides studies of Disney, the Super Bowl, *Marcus Welby,* and Billy Graham, along with material of theoretical importance.

Rosenberg, Bernard, & White, David Manning. (Eds.). (1957). *Mass culture: The popular arts in America*. New York: Free Press. This is one of the earliest and most important collections of articles on the subject of mass culture.

Tuchman, Gaye, Daniels, Arlene Kaplan, & Benét, James. (Eds.). (1978). *Hearth and home: Images of women in the mass media*. New York: Oxford University Press. This book contains articles on images of women in television and women's magazines, and includes an extensive annotated bibliography on the subject.

Weibel, Kathryn. (1977). *Mirror mirror: Images of women reflected in popular culture*. Garden City, NY: Anchor. This book deals with images of women found in fiction, television, the movies, women's magazines, print advertising, and fashion.

Wilson, Robert N. (Ed.). (1964). *The arts in society*. Englewood Cliffs, NJ: Prentice Hall. This book focuses on high culture, but it includes some excellent articles of interest to media analysts, including two by Ian Watt (on Robinson Crusoe and on literature and society).

PART II

Applications

<u>Murder on the Orient Express</u> and classical murder mysteries in general are examined in this chapter from semiotic and Marxist points of view. The chapter includes discussion of how Agatha Christie violates the "code" of the single murderer and how mysteries are, in fact, problems in applied semiotics that readers or viewers often cannot solve because they either neglect or misinterpret the signifiers (clues) that are provided. The elements of class conflict found in mysteries are also discussed, as well as the role these elements may play in diverting people's attention and mystifying them. Finally, it is suggested that, ironically, mysteries may have a revolutionary element implicit in their structure.

CHAPTER 5

Murderers on the
Orient Express

Murder on the Orient Express is generally considered to be one of Agatha Christie's best works and a classic in the analytic detective mystery genre. It was also made into a highly successful movie that used the story primarily as a vehicle for cameo roles by major stars such as Lauren Bacall and Ingrid Bergman, but that also was beautifully acted and wonderfully absorbing.

What is distinctive about this particular story is that, unlike in most mysteries, *all* of the suspects were the actual murderers. And once Hercule Poirot figured this out, everything else fell beautifully into place—as things must in a well-constructed mystery. A mystery story is, semiotically speaking, like a coded message. All kinds of signs and significations are observable, but the connections among them are not obvious. Once we see how they are related and "break the code," the mystery is solved. Clues, then, are signifiers with a number of different signifieds. We must assemble these clues and interpret them properly to make sense of things and find the killer(s).

In *Murder on the Orient Express*, Christie's decision to create a dozen suspects who are all guilty was a remarkable and ingenious structural innovation, a reversal of the conventional situation in which only one suspect is guilty. The fascination of watching the movie or reading the story lies in seeing how Poirot puts everything together. Many of the people who have seen the film probably previously read the book; often readers want to see a book they have enjoyed actualized on film—to see it "come alive," reinterpreted—and in this case that is what the film's viewers get.

ORGANIZING A MYSTERY

If we forget (to the extent this is possible) about the actual plot and examine the story in terms of characters and relationships, we find that *Murder on the Orient Express* has a very symmetrical organization. There are three main characters—or, rather, two characters who are polar opposites and a group of a dozen other interrelated characters who form a third character and who mediate between the first two. We find Poirot, the detective, on one side and Ratchett (an alias for a kidnapper, Cassetti) on the other. By chance, Poirot happens to board the Orient Express on his way back to France with Ratchett and a dozen other people. Ratchett recognizes Poirot and, because Ratchett has received some death threats, he offers Poirot $20,000 to protect him. But Poirot has taken an immediate and instinctive dislike to Ratchett, and so refuses.

Ratchett looks "evil" and Poirot, Christie tells us, looks comic. He is described as "a ridiculous-looking little man. The sort of little man one could never take seriously." In addition to Ratchett and Poirot, there are a dozen assorted passengers of varying classes and nationalities on the Orient Express.

At the very beginning of the book, on the first day of the trip, Poirot is speculating with a friend, Monsieur Bouc, over lunch. Bouc has been "studying" the people on board the train:

> "Ah!" he sighed. "If I had but the pen of a Balzac! I would depict this scene." He waved a hand.
>
> "It is an idea, that," said Poirot.
>
> "Ah, you agree? It has not been done. I think? And yet—it lends itself to romance, my friend. All around us are people, of all classes, of all nationalities, of all ages. For three days these people, these strangers to one another, are brought together. They sleep and eat under one roof, they cannot get away from each other. At the end of three days

they part, they go their several ways, never perhaps to see each other again."

"And yet," said Poirot, "suppose an accident—"

"Ah, no, my friend—"

"From your point of view it would be regrettable, I agree. But nevertheless let us just for one moment suppose it. Then, perhaps, all these here are linked together—by death."

This leads Poirot to examine rather carefully the 13 other persons on the train, all of whom are dining at the time, and to speculate about them. The fact of the matter is that all of the characters *are* linked together by death—by the various tragedies ensuing from Cassetti/Ratchett's kidnapping of a child, Daisy Armstrong, in the United States in the distant past. And it is this link, which is dangled before the reader several times in the story, that is the key to solving the mystery.

Let us look at the characters in terms of their relationships. The following lists present some interesting paradigmatic oppositions:

Poirot	12 murderers on the train	Ratchett
discovers killers	all kill (stab) Ratchett	is killed
refuses to work for Ratchett	all connected to Ratchett and become involved with Poirot	asks Poirot to work for him
looks ridiculous	all look different	looks evil

The puzzle in the story involves discovering how the 12 seemingly random characters on the train are connected. Had Ratchett discerned that they were connected, he might have lived. When Poirot discovers they are connected, he finds the murderers—though, curiously enough, he lets them go. He is able to do this because he is provided (by the murderers) with an acceptable explanation or counterexplanation of the murder, and he chooses to accept this alternative, which involves a mysterious stranger who supposedly left the train after Ratchett's murder.

Once Poirot recognizes that some of the occupants of the train were involved in the Armstrong case, he is able eventually to link all 12 characters together. Toward the end of the book, but before it is revealed that all 12 occupants of the train are "related," we find the following bit of dialogue:

"Nothing would surprise me now."

"Nothing! Even if everybody in the train proved to have been in the Armstrong household, I should not express surprise."

"This is a very profound remark," said Poirot.

We do not at the time recognize the significance of this remark, but Bouc has accidentally stumbled upon the solution to the mystery, and Christie has him offer it to us, knowing that we will not take it seriously. When we look back at the end of the story, we discover that Christie has given us all we needed to know to solve the mystery, but we have either neglected or misinterpreted all the clues. That is, we either neglected important signifiers or misinterpreted them and ended up with the wrong signifieds.

DETECTIVES AS SEMIOTICIANS

Murder mysteries fascinate us because they involve, ultimately, decoding a series of clues—signs and significations (actions, words, objects) that seem random, irrelevant, or both, and that are meaningless until we find the code that ties everything together. The great detectives of analytic murder fiction are semioticians, whether they know it or not. And the pleasure we derive from reading mysteries stems in part from the semiotic problems they pose—the puzzles that we all try to figure out.

The resolution to the story in *Murder on the Orient Express* comes when Poirot seizes upon the tale of the fictitious murderer as a means of enabling the real murderers to escape punishment. This resolution is itself connected to certain moral codes we have, such as the notion that evildoers "deserve" to be punished for their crimes and that, in the right circumstances, a sufficiently evil character should be murdered. The dilemma faced by this unusual group of vigilantes (for that's what they were, though some of them were cloaked in European finery) is the dilemma faced by all such groups: How do you justify lawlessness—in this case murder—in the name of law and order? Poirot's response is an emotional one, which may suggest, as psychoanalytic literature so amply demonstrates, that there are forces aside from "little gray cells" that influence the actions of men and women.

The classical murder mystery is a subcategory of the murder mystery genre in which rationality and logic are stressed and in which there is a primal confrontation between the emotion, irrationality, and hatred of the murderer (who must also be extremely devious and calculating) and the mind of the detective. This genre is highly formulaic and includes many conventions that must be observed if the mystery is to be legitimate. A good classical mystery, then, involves a confrontation between two minds.

It has been suggested by some Freudian analysts that the fascination with murder mysteries is connected to children's frustrated desires to know what is going on in their parents' bedrooms; they assert that adults transfer these desires to other locked doors and mysterious sounds in the night.

SOCIAL AND
POLITICAL DIMENSIONS

Murder on the Orient Express, both the book and the film, may also be examined in terms of social and political dimensions. The characters are all linked together, but not by what should join people together—love and a sense of community. Rather, they are linked by hatred and death. However, this escape from an alienated and estranged relationship is only momentary. When the Orient Express arrives in France, all the passengers will go their separate ways, with only memories of a ritual murder to bind them together.

Ironically, however, the book does suggest the possibility of a society based not on class differences and estrangement but on a communality of interest—on common goals that all men and women share. The inversion in *Murder on the Orient Express* is interesting because it demonstrates that members of different classes can work together when they see it is in their interest to do so. Class differences can be overcome.

Of course, we must always keep in mind the fact that Cassetti/Ratchett had kidnapped the child of a wealthy family, and it might be argued that the poor and working-class characters serve, ultimately, as instruments of the wealthy (and even royal) elements among the murderers. Cassetti/Ratchett had, we know, "touched" the lives of all involved, but it is the insistence, we may presume, of the upper-class people involved that has brought everyone together, remarkably, on the Orient Express. And it is the very existence of social, national, and class differences that everyone counts on to confuse anyone who might be suspicious.

It might be argued that the "mystification" the murderers create parallels the social mystification that the bourgeoisie finds so important to maintain itself.

A mystery story, in its own way, is a kind of microcosm of the larger society. Perhaps it is no accident that so many mysteries—especially the classical English ones involving deduction—feature people from the wealthy and aristocratic levels of society as killers, rather than having "the butler do it." This would suggest class conflict too overtly. There are, of course, many mysteries that include class strife and conflict between the poor and the rich, but many also involve only intra-upper-class murder, a sign of the degeneracy of the bourgeoisie. Ironically, the murders in these stories are usually solved by detectives who come from working-class and middle-class backgrounds, so an element of class conflict is still visible in these works.

POIROT AS REVOLUTIONARY

In a strange way, then, characters such as Poirot may be said to have a revolutionary dimension, though their efforts are focused on the personal, not the societal, level and they function most immediately as instruments of official bourgeois social morality.

Behind our fascination with the wealthy and their glamorous self-indulgent lifestyles, there is a germ of hostility and resentment and a sense of relative deprivation that has political (and even revolutionary) implications. At the same time, mysteries serve as diversions; they take our attention away from the real world and our problems and offer us characters, many of whom are vile and degenerate, who ultimately pay for their crimes. Thus they function as sacrificial victims, enabling us to purge ourselves (somewhat) of hostile feelings toward the rich and powerful.

Instead of a real revolution against the real bourgeoisie, we "kill off" the rich one by one in mystery stories. But these are the imaginary rich, and so our hostility (and its revolutionary potential) is dissipated. This might be the ultimate form of mystification, in which imaginary confrontations between a potentially revolutionary proletariat, symbolized by the detective and police, and the bourgeoisie are all acted out in fantasy.

One other thing we learn from mysteries such as *Murder on the Orient Express*: We, the common people, lack the intelligence and wisdom to solve such mysteries; by implication, we may be unqualified to run our own social and political institutions. We are reduced, psychologically, to children who do not understand what really is going on. The implication of these stories is that we are better off entrusting the control of society to those who are wiser and more powerful than we, which is exactly what the bourgeoisie wants the masses to believe (that is, the status quo is functional).

Although the murder mystery is a commodity manufactured to be sold to the largest possible market, and although the mystery generally acts as an instrument of false consciousness (which distracts people from their real interests), it may also, ironically, have a revolutionary potential. This is because many of the murders found in this genre are committed by members of the upper classes and show the degeneracy of these people. Replacing them, then, seems quite reasonable. The murders also reveal the vulnerability of the upper classes; they cannot be protected from their fates despite their huge homes, servants, and so on. Thus every murder has political implications and dimensions in spite of itself, and every murderer, without knowing it, helps break the iron grip that the "classes" have upon the consciousness of the "masses."

Many of the murders that take place in these classical mysteries suggest, even if vaguely, the possibility of revolutionary violence; they play a role, even if in an oblique manner, in the class struggle. (Actually, in the classical English murder mysteries, the upper class seems to be killing itself off in rapid fashion. Eventually, we may surmise, there will be nothing left but the working class, whose members will be surprised to discover that the upper class has, bit by bit, destroyed itself, so there is no need for a revolution.) Agatha Christie would be astonished at such notions. Poirot, of course, would not find them surprising at all.

STUDY QUESTIONS AND TOPICS FOR DISCUSSION

1. What are the oppositions in *Murder on the Orient Express*? How do
   they generate "meaning" in the text?
2. Which characterization of Poirot seems more reasonable—Poirot as
   semiotician or Poirot as revolutionary? Justify your answer.

In this chapter, football is described from a semiotic viewpoint, as a system of signs, with emphasis on the various sign subsystems (uniforms of the players, officials, and cheerleaders; sign sections in the stands; and so on). Special attention is paid to time and its manipulation by teams and by television broadcasters using the instant replay camera. The chapter then turns to the socializing function of football and its role in preparing people to work in a specialized and bureaucratic society—in particular, in the corporate world. Football is contrasted with baseball, which is described as a 19th-century pastoral game, no longer synchronous with Americans' "hopped-up" and time-bound sensibilities. Football is also described, sociologically speaking, as a functional alternative to organized religion. A Marxist interpretation of the game is also offered, focusing on football's role as a diversion, the treatment of players as commodities, and the business aspects of the game, especially in regard to television advertising.

CHAPTER 6

Seven Points on
the Game of Football

FOOTBALL IS A GAME OF SIGNS

Football is an interesting subject for the semiotician because the game is simultaneously full of signs and a signifier of some importance. The stadium is itself one huge sign—a sacred space where enthusiasts (and sometimes fanatics) gather to watch a highly organized, ritualized contest that many have suggested functions as an alternative to war. It is not unusual for 60,000 people or more to gather together for a game, and with television coverage sometimes millions of people watch a game, which means that the entire country "becomes" a football stadium.

Where an individual sits in the stadium—on the 50-yard line or way up behind a goalpost—is a signifier of wealth, power, or status. The field itself is a huge grid, a 100-yard rectangle of white lines against brilliant green grass (or Astroturf). The intensity of the colors adds considerably to the excitement of the event and must not be underestimated. On and around the field are people in all kinds of different uniforms: the officials in their zebra stripes, the players with their helmets and pads, members of marching bands, cheerleaders and pom-pom girls in sweaters and miniskirts, coaches with earphones and other electronic paraphernalia, drum majors and majorettes, and many other people. All of the uniforms and trappings of these participants are signifiers of the wide variety of skills, activities, and functions taking place at a game: rule enforcement, athletic activity, musical diversion, sexual display, planning and rationality, and so on. Thus a football game is not merely an athletic event, but part of a much larger system of events that are connected to the game but that enlarge its significance greatly.

(I have not said anything about the people who attend the games and who frequently wear the colors or emblems of their teams. Sometimes they carry signs. Frequently there are "sign sections" in stadiums, especially at college games, and they flash various messages during halftime, when the bands play and there are other entertainments.)

The game of football itself is based on signs. Signals are called in the huddles to announce offensive plays. These signals are analogous to what semioticians call codes (see Chapter 1); they indicate a precise series of activities that are to be followed at given points in time. Defensive players learn to watch their opponents for indications that a pass is to be thrown or a certain play is to be run. And a good deal of the game is based on *deception*—that is, giving opponents false signifiers so they will make mistakes. It is the capacity of signs to lie, to give false information, that creates much of the complexity found in football.

The officials also use signs—a variety of gestures that indicate what rules have been violated and the penalties assessed. These signals are actually nonverbal, visual metaphors that enable officials to indicate to everyone in the stadium the nature of a given transgression. The sign that is most important, the one in which an official stretches both hands over his head to indicate a score, is a signifier with two signifieds: triumph or success for the offensive team and failure for the defensive team. When this sign is given, thousands and thousands of people in the stadium (and in the television audience) cheer madly or groan.

While the game progresses, there is a great deal of activity taking place on the sidelines. During college games, bands play rousing songs at certain times to encourage their teams, and cheerleaders lead cheers, jump up and down (displaying their breasts and legs), and carry on, often in rather mechanical dancing and movement displays. Many professional football teams employ groups of attractive young women who "wiggle and jiggle" on the sidelines, indicating that there is a sexual dimension to the game or, more precisely, to the spectacle in which the game is embedded.

INSTANT REPLAY AND
THE MODERN SENSIBILITY

As the various subsystems that are part of the spectacle of football work themselves out, there is one sign that is crucial to the understanding of what football means—in its televised form, in particular—and that is the huge scoreboard clock. Time is of the essence in football, but, unlike in baseball and other sports, in football time can be manipulated. And it is this manipulation of time in tightly fought games that generates incredible tension in the sport.

In a one-sided game there is little tension, and the game often turns into an exhibition of power and competence for the winning team and a study in humiliation for the losing one. But in close games, time is everyone's enemy. The winning team fights to hold on to its advantage and the losing one tries to use what time is left to best advantage and to score. Many football games are decided in the last minutes and often even in the last seconds of play. A minute of playing time, because of the rules of the game, can take many minutes of real time.

What further complicates matters, especially in televised games, is the use of instant replay, which can show a given play from a variety of different perspectives and suggests, ultimately, that time doesn't pass in football the way it does in real life. We keep seeing the past (a given play) over and over again from different angles, so that our sense of continuity and perspective are rendered problematic. Time doesn't pass the way we thought it did, and we see that our perspective on the world isn't the only one.

Televised football has become an incredibly sophisticated art form. It now may be said to resemble avant-garde films, in that both often simulate stream-of-consciousness thought, which moves backward and forward in time, jumping around almost incoherently at times. Instant replay is vaguely equivalent to the flashback in film, and the invention of instant replay has dramatically altered the nature of televised football (and other sports as well) in particular and the modern American sensibility in general. In Super Bowl XVI, between the San Francisco 49ers and the Cincinnati Bengals, CBS used 16 cameras on the field to televise the game and another 7 for locker-room shows and other activities. It had 14 videotape machines for instant replays, which meant that an incredible number of perspectives was possible on every play.

Can anyone doubt that a new sensibility arises out of seeing such programming? Or at least that a new sensibility is made possible because of the development of such a remarkable kind of program?

FOOTBALL SOCIALIZES US

Football does more than just entertain us. The word *entertain* is like the word *interesting*, in that neither tells us very much. The questions we should ask about football include the following: Why do we find football so entertaining? What do we get out of the game? What does it do *for* us (that is, what gratifications does it offer)? What might it be doing *to* us? What does it tell us about American society?

One very important aspect of football is the way it socializes and enculturates us. It teaches us how to get along in society, what roles to play, what rules to follow, what life is all about, and so on. We are not aware that this is going on most of the time, which means that we are all the more susceptible to the influence of what the game suggests, teaches, and implies. In this section we will look at the game as a signifier of values, attitudes, and beliefs and attempt to ascertain what these signifieds are and what effects they may have upon people (admittedly, this is a speculative activity).

One thing we learn from examining football is that we live in a highly complex society in which time is critical and communication is important. A good deal of the game involves communication between coaching staff and players. Signals are called on both sides for every play. Nothing is done that has not been planned, rehearsed, and prepared over and over again in practice sessions. It is only the fact that people make mistakes, or do things that cannot be anticipated, that messes up the plans of coaches.

In addition, we learn that society is highly specialized, and that this specialization functions within group situations. Teams are now made up of offensive and defensive specialists, each with particular talents and abilities. Football teams function as "models" for modern society, and we learn from watching football that we must be specialists working in highly structured organizations, controlled from above (the coaches), and that we must pursue our specializations for the good of the group, first and foremost, and then for ourselves. That's what it means to be a "team player." We learn from football, without being aware of it, that we must prepare ourselves to function in a highly bureaucratic society—most likely within a large corporate entity. Watching football is "training" for working in the corporate world, and the violence in football is transformed into sales campaigns aimed at "smashing" the public, one's competitors, or both.

We also learn that specialization and ability constitute a means of upward mobility, especially in professional football, where farm boys, Blacks from working-class families, and others who have never before been wealthy often earn huge salaries. Many youngsters identify very strongly with football stars, whose heroics on the football field are, at times, quite incredible.

In a sense, football is really about containment and breaking free, about order and randomness—though always within the context of the game (which is highly structured and rule dominated). These moments of freedom are exciting and highly exhilarating, but they are fleeting and quite unpredictable. It is not too much of an oversimplification to say that much of football is routine and boring, and that what makes the game so exciting is that there are moments when remarkable things happen. Because we can never know when one of these great plays will happen, we must pay attention all the time, lest we miss something.

WHY BASEBALL IS BORING

The reason we find football so exciting is that it closely approximates and reflects the contemporary social situation in the United States. Football is a 20th-century sport for people who live in a world in which time is precious (time is money), communication is important (we live in an "information" society), and bureaucratic entities are dominant (corporations, universities, and so on). Baseball, on the other hand, is a 19th-century pastoral sport in which time is irrelevant, specialization is not crucial, and there is relatively little reliance on plays and

Curiously enough, as religions (especially liberal religions) have become more rational and have continued to *demythologize* themselves, football has become more arcane and mysterious, with incredibly complex plays and tactics that function much the way theology does for religion. People seem to have a need for myth, ritual, mystery, and heroism, and football, perhaps more than religion in contemporary societies, is helping people satisfy these needs.

Whether the messages we get from football are as valuable and positive as those we get from sermons and other aspects of religion is another matter, and one that bears thinking about. Has football become "the opiate of the people"? There are some who hold that belief, and it is to their interpretation that we now turn.

THE MARXIST PERSPECTIVE

Football games, held in huge stadiums, with bands, cheerleaders, halftime shows, and so on, are spectacles par excellence. The function of these spectacles (that is, the latent function), it may be argued, is to divert people's attention from their real social situation, to drain them of their emotional energy (which might have been expended on political and social issues), and, ultimately, to convince them of the justness of the political order. A political system that can provide good football is worth keeping. And because football also trains us for our place in the modern, corporate, capitalist world, it is doubly valuable.

The great gatherings that are held in the United States are not generally held for political purposes, though at times this does happen. Instead, Americans gather together to watch spectacles—of which football is an important exemplar. It isn't hard to see a parallel between the old Roman principle of bread and circuses—to divert the mobs from their misery—and what goes on in the United States on Fridays (high school games), Saturdays (college games), and Sundays (professional games), as well as Monday nights on television.

Is the intensity of our interest in football a measure of the alienation we feel in our everyday lives—lives in which we sense a radical separation from our possibilities, in which we feel hemmed in by huge bureaucratic structures that dominate our work lives and by the competitiveness that characterizes our social order? The less satisfying our lives, the more bothered we are by the "rat race," the more we turn to vicarious satisfactions like football and, curiously, the less psychic nourishment we get from them. Ironically, football is itself essentially routine and boring, and it teaches us, though we generally are not aware of it, that we must learn how to accommodate ourselves to the society in which we live.

Football, especially professional football, is a huge business that exists for one purpose: to make money. It treats players as commodities—objects to be sold and traded, almost at whim (though unionization has modified this a good deal). Players also have little sense of loyalty. They see the huge profits the team owners make and they fight to be paid huge salaries—all that the market can bear. The ultimate irony is that it is television that benefits most from the existence of football, and television uses football for its main purpose—as filler between commercials. Television, as it exists in the United States, is a business that makes money by selling commercial time. Football attracts large audiences and costs relatively little to produce (compared, say, with crime shows or documentaries), so it is very cost-effective.

Thus we have a situation in which everyone is exploiting or trying to exploit everyone else, and the result of all this is that spectacles are produced that people use to obtain vicarious excitement and pleasure and that have the hidden functions of teaching people to accept the status quo and to accommodate themselves to corporations and the political order.

The potential for revolutionary violence in the masses is siphoned off as people watch linemen battle one another in the trenches and defensive players hit halfbacks and cornerbacks. After a weekend of football, the heavy viewer will have participated vicariously in enough violence to fuel a dozen revolutions.

A look at the rosters of football teams shows that Blacks are heavily and disproportionately represented. This is an indication of the fact that Black people suffer more from our economic system than Whites do and thus need football (as well as boxing and other sports) as an instrument of social mobility. For poor Black kids, football is a means of escaping from poverty and achieving middle-class status—at least for a while. To be successful, however, one must learn to fit in—to adopt essentially bourgeois values, such as being a team player, not causing trouble, and respecting authority figures. A player, no matter how talented, who causes problems and doesn't follow the rules will not prosper in college or professional football. Thus there is a price to be paid by players—namely, *accommodation*, which leads the way to *co-optation.*

FOOTBALL AND THE PSYCHE

I have suggested that football functions as a means of socializing people and of diverting their attention from their real concerns. I would also like to suggest that football is vitally connected with particular unconscious processes, which explains, in part, the powerful hold football has on people. If large numbers of people read the comics or watch football or do anything, quite likely it is because these things provide them with important psychic gratifications, even though the people may not be aware of them.

For one thing, there is the matter of violence in football. The controlled violence of football may satisfy two contradictory desires: the desire to be violent and the desire to be under control, so that violence doesn't overwhelm us. Violence is integral to the game of football; every play involves blocks, hits, tackles, or the like. Our attraction to violence stems from a number of sources, such as the fact that we must restrain our impulsive behavior, and the fact that we are all involved (unconsciously) in Oedipal problems, sibling rivalries, and so on. Quite likely the matter of sexual repression is important; violence can become a kind of substitute gratification. (There is a connection, also, between violence and eroticism that must be kept in mind. There is a sexual dimension to violence just as there is an aggressive and violent dimension to sexuality.)

The violence in football may also help men to form a masculine identity. We live in an information society, in which processing data and communicating account for a dominant part of the gross national product. In such a society, men find it hard to develop a male identity, especially given that American male identity has historically been connected to a 19th-century lifestyle—cutting wood, herding cattle, doing hard physical labor. Watching violence on the football field becomes one of the few ways in which American men can help themselves form a male identity, even if the violence is vicarious and potentially destructive.

Football lends itself to a number of interpretations of a psychoanalytic nature. For example, we can interpret the game as mirroring the battles among id, ego, and superego forces in the human psyche:

Id	*Ego*	*Superego*
offensive team	officials	defensive team
drives	rules	prevention

In football, the offensive team wants to have long drives and to score; the defensive team wants to stop these drives and get control of the ball; and the officials function as an ego, to keep the game going.

Arnold J. Mandell (1974), a psychiatrist who spent some time with the San Diego Chargers, has categorized professional football players as follows:

Position	*Personality Traits*
offensive linemen	ambitious, tenacious, precise, attentive to detail
wide receivers	narcissistic, vain, loners
quarterbacks	self-confident, courageous
defensive linemen	restless, peevish, irritable, intolerant of detail, uninhibited, wild
linebackers	controlled, brutal, internally conflicted

Mandell found that players need particular personality traits in order to be able to play their positions. For example, he discovered that offensive players on the Chargers kept their lockers neat and orderly, whereas the lockers of defensive players were invariably messy.

> It became clear that offensive football players like structure and discipline. They want to maintain the status quo. They tend to be conservative as people, and as football players they take comfort in repetitious practice of well-planned and well-executed plays. The defensive players, just as clearly, can't stand structure; their attitudes, their behavior and their life-styles bear this out. (Mandell, 1974, p. 12)

All of this is important because, more than anything else, according to Mandell, "the game is in the mind"; this is probably true of all games.

CONCLUDING REMARKS

Although football might seem to be only a simple entertainment, it is actually a matter of some consequence from a number of points of view. We use language from football in our political discourse; the football season creates lamentable "football widows" every fall; the game is played by children, adolescents, college students, and grown men; it is an industry; it has a long history—I could go on endlessly. Football is a subject that attracts a great deal of attention from the general public and one that deserves attention from the media analyst.

But there is something else to be said here that every media analyst must remember. When examining programs carried by the media—whether the focus is football, soap operas, news, or any other genre—analysts must never forget that they are dealing with art forms, and art forms are extremely complicated phenomena. The media analyst must be careful not to reduce any program to nothing but a system of signs, nothing but a socializing agent, nothing but a means of manipulating people's consciousness, nothing but a subject in which drives, Oedipal problems, and the like are manifested. The analyst must somehow analyze each program from a number of different points of view and still respect it as a creative effort (even if not a very successful one) and a work of art that has performance aspects, aesthetic elements, and more. To be a media analyst, an individual must know all kinds of things and, in a sense, know everything at the same time.

STUDY QUESTIONS AND TOPICS FOR DISCUSSION

1. Discuss football in terms of the following perspectives: a semiotic sign system, an avant-garde art form, a means of socializing people, a bourgeois capitalist enterprise, and a religion of sorts.
2. What do psychoanalytic investigations of football and football players reveal? (What significance may there be in football's obsession with penetrating end zones?)
3. Compare football with baseball and explain why many people find baseball boring.

According to the Russian semiotician Yuri Lotman, every aspect of a work of art is important. Taking this notion as a point of departure, this chapter analyzes in detail a print advertisement for Fidji perfume, considering 17 different semiotic signs found in the ad. The advertisement is also analyzed paradigmatically; that is, the polar oppositions that it suggests are discussed. In addition, a psychoanalytic interpretation of the advertisement and its symbols is offered. Finally, an aside on moisturizers and women's fears is followed by a brief discussion of perfume and anxiety.

CHAPTER 7

The Maiden With the Snake

Interpretations of a
Print Advertisement

Hamlet:	Do you see yonder cloud that's almost in shape of a camel?
Polonius:	By the mass, and 'tis like a camel, indeed.
Hamlet:	Methinks it is like a weasel.
Polonius:	It is backed like a weasel.
Hamlet:	Or like a whale?
Polonius:	Very like a whale.

William Shakespeare, *Hamlet*, act III, scene ii

In this chapter I will offer interpretations of a remarkable print advertisement for Fidji perfume from the perspectives of semiotic analysis, paradigmatic analysis, and psychoanalytic theory.

SIGNS IN SIGNS: A PRIMER ON APPLIED SEMIOTICS

I would like to offer an analogy that might be useful here. Think of yourself, when acting as a "practicing semiotician," as being like Sherlock Holmes or some other detective investigating a crime. The detective is looking for clues, and everything is potentially significant. Remember what Peirce said: "The universe is perfused with signs, if not made up entirely of them" (quoted in Zeman, 1977). And as Yuri Lotman (1977) has explained, everything in a work of art is important.

The difference between the detectives in crime novels and the readers of those novels is that the detectives don't miss important signs that readers gloss over. In novels, these important signs are frequently buried in descriptions, to which readers ordinarily pay little attention.

So, let me ask—what might be important in a print advertisement or a radio or television commercial? What is important in any text? (In scholarly discourse about works of art of all kinds, the subjects of analysis are generally referred to as *texts*.) The answer—Peirce would tell us—is everything!

It is possible to make a distinction between the sign/advertisement and the signs, semiotically speaking, found in the advertisement. For purposes of this discussion of advertisements from a semiotic perspective, it will be useful to think of each signifier within an ad as an elemental sign or *signeme*—a fundamental sign that cannot be broken down any further. For example, a bottle of champagne is in itself a sign, but within that sign are such signemes as bubbles, foil, the cork, and the way the champagne gushes out of the bottle after it's been opened.

Following is a list of important nonverbal signemes. This list does not, of course, cover all possible signemes to be found in print advertisements, television commercials, or any other visual texts, but it suggests some of the most commonly found signemes. Depending upon the particular text, all of these signemes can have varying degrees of importance.

hair color	earrings and other body adornments
hairstyle	setting
eye color	relationships implied
facial structure	spatiality
body type	occupations
age	activities going on
gender	background
race	lighting
facial expression	sound effects, music
body language	typefaces in text
makeup	design
clothes	color
style of eyeglasses	

Verbal signemes may include the following:

words used	arguments and appeals made
questions asked	slogans
metaphors and similes	headlines
associations (metonymy)	paradoxes generated
negations made	tone
affirmations offered	style

Keep in mind that a word is a kind of sign, and that the definition of a word is based on convention and must be learned. This is, at least in part, why dictionaries are always being revised.

THE MAIDEN IN PARADISE: A CASE STUDY

Let's take an interesting print advertisement as a case study in applied semiotic analysis. The advertisement we will examine, for Fidji perfume, appeared a number of years ago in many fashion magazines (see Figure 7.1, which reproduces the ad, which appeared in magazines in color, in black and white).

The ad features a photograph that shows part of the face of an apparently Polynesian woman (from just below her nose) who is holding a bottle of Fidji perfume in her curiously intertwined fingers. Her fingernails are red. She has long, dark hair, full red lips (slightly parted), and a yellow orchid is tucked into her hair near her right ear (on the left of the photo). Around the woman's neck is a snake, part of whose body forms something that looks like an infinity symbol. The snake's head points downward, slightly covering the top of the perfume bottle. The lighting is rather dramatic, using chiaroscuro (which means, in essence, both clear and dark): Parts of the photograph are light, whereas other parts, particularly the upper right, are quite dark.

Below, I list and briefly discuss some of the things a semiotician might write about in interpreting this advertisement.

The formal design of the ad. In the minds of most Americans, formal design (approximating axial balance), simplicity, and spaciousness (a great deal of white or "empty" space) are associated with wealth and

Figure 7.1. Advertisement for Fidji Perfume

sophistication. Advertisements for expensive and "classy" products often are full of white space—that is, they are relatively empty.

The warm colors. The ad shows a yellow orchid in the woman's hair and full red lips and fingernails. Red is commonly used to suggest passion.

The partial showing of the woman's face. Because only the bottom part of the woman's face, from just above her lips, is visible, it is possible for women viewing the ad to identify with her more easily than if her complete face were shown. The woman's lips are partly open; open lips often are used to suggest sexual excitement or passion. Further, the lighting emphasizes her long and slender neck.

The woman's ethnicity. In the popular imagination, Polynesia is connected with fantasies of natural love and sexuality. The French painter Gauguin abandoned France for Polynesia, and many people are familiar with the story of his "escape" to paradise, where people are not burdened with rules and prohibitions (civilization and its discontents).

The woman's hair. Dark hair, in American culture, is often associated with warmth, heat, and sexual passion. Women with blonde hair, on the other hand, are often thought of as Nordic and cold, or as innocent and sexually unresponsive. The woman's hair is long, also—something frequently connected in the popular mind with youth and sexual abandon. (This explains all those commercials with young women, their long hair flying in the breeze, running through meadows toward—presumably—their lovers.) It is quite common for women to cut their hair short when they get older, so they don't have to bother with it as much.

The name of the perfume. The name Fidji makes the connection between the perfume and Polynesia (and all the connotations that go with it) explicit. The copy in the advertisement reinforces this notion.

The yellow orchid. Flowers are the sexual apparatus of a plant, so there is a hint of sexuality in the use of the orchid, which, due to the lighting, is prominently displayed. Also, *flowering* is a word often used to describe a woman's becoming physically developed, and with that, sexually receptive. Flowers are signs of love. Orchids are thought of as rare and delicate and are associated with the tropics.

The snake. According to Freudian theory, snakes are phallic symbols by virtue of their shape—an example of iconicity that is used in both semiotic and psychoanalytic interpretation. (I should note that in some countries, a similar advertisement appeared for this perfume, but without the snake.) This image, a woman with a snake around her neck (it has been suggested that it looks like a corn snake) is also found in Piero di Cosimo's portrait of Simonetta Vespucci and other works of art as well—an example of intertextuality (as discussed in Chapter 1), the conscious or unconscious borrowing from one work for another.

The relationship between women and snakes goes back a long way, to the Garden of Eden, and the outcome of that relationship, Adam's temptation, has been of considerable importance in Western history. One might argue that the snake in the story of the Garden of Eden is the prototypical advertising executive. According to Genesis, "The serpent was more subtle than any beast in the field which the Lord God had made," and he convinced Eve that if she ate from the tree of knowledge of good and evil she wouldn't die but her eyes would be opened. After she ate from the tree and convinced Adam to do the same, they were both thrown out of the Garden of Eden, and all kinds of things followed from that expulsion. Eve's excuse was "The serpent beguiled me, and I did eat." Advertising executives have been beguiling the progeny of Adam and Eve ever since then—though they have not been required to slide on their bellies and eat dust.

Another association with snakes is found in the Greek myth of Medusa, one of the Gorgons, whose hair was made of snakes. Any man who looked upon Medusa turned to stone. Hair, this myth suggests, has power.

The intertwined fingers. The woman's fingers are intertwined in a rather curious way, with a finger of one hand shown poking between two fingers of the other hand—giving the vague impression of a penis coming between two legs. We find intertwined fingers in some well-known works of art, such as Alessandro Botticelli's *Primavera*, so there is another intertextual relationship that might be considered.

The bottle. The perfume bottle has a large stopper and is shown with strong highlights that run across it. A vertical black line runs down the middle of the bottle and a horizontal black ribbon is wrapped around the neck of the bottle, below the stopper.

The woman's nakedness. The woman is not wearing any clothes, which reinforces the photo's paradisiacal image. Before Adam and Eve ate from the tree of knowledge, they were naked, and nakedness is associated in Western consciousness with innocence (and in the case of nudists, for example, with a desire to regain the innocence of paradise). Curiously enough, we do not see any indication of the woman's breasts—they seem to have been airbrushed out. Showing breasts might suggest maternity and related matters, which would not be conducive to fantasies of primordial sex with a natural (read "uninhibited") woman. Showing breasts is much different, I would argue, from showing cleavage and subtly indicating breasts—which is a sexual turn-on for men.

The use of French. The text of the ad is all in French, which is undoubtedly used because of its metonymic qualities—because Americans tend to associate the French with style, sophistication, and sexiness (whether any of these associations reflect reality is beside the point). The French language also acts as a means of separating those with refinement and "class," who know French (or at least can understand the French that is used in this advertisement—which is not very difficult), from the "masses."

The copy. In the upper right-hand corner of the advertisement, in relatively small type, we see "<u>Fidji</u>: le parfum des paradis retrouvés." I would translate this as "Fidji: the perfume of paradise regained (or rediscovered)." You really don't have to know French to understand most of the headline. The key French that it helps to know is *retrouvés*. The phrase "paradise regained" is one that people with any degree of education are familiar with. So even if they don't know what *retrouvés* means, they can most likely figure it out. Thus a person doesn't really have to know French or be particularly "sophisticated" to be able to understand the headline.

On the bottle, the words "Parfums Guy Laroche Paris" appear, along with the Fidji logo. The only other verbiage is at the bottom of the ad, on a light band below the image of the woman and the snake, which reads in a roman face "Fidji de Guy Laroche," and then in small italics, "*De la Haute Couture à la Haute Parfumerie*," which translates, roughly, as "From High Fashion to High Perfume."

There is, then, rather little in the way of copy in this ad. The image of the woman and the snake is used to sell Fidji, rather than any verbal arguments. This style is rather common in perfume ads, because they are selling, in one way or another, fantasies of sexual abandon, paradisiacal sex, and similar notions.

The "hidden word." The curves of the snake's body can be seen as forming the letter *S*; the highlights on the top of the bottle's stopper, on the top of the bottle itself, and on the bottom of the bottle can be seen as an *E*; and the woman's fingers clearly form an *X*. Thus the word *sex* is hidden, or embedded, in the image and, so some scholars argue, even though people who look at the advertisement may not consciously see the word hidden in the image, they pick it up unconsciously and are affected by it.

The crucifix. The vertical black line on the bottle and the horizontal ribbon at the bottle's neck may be seen as a highly stylized crucifix form, a bit of symbology that possibly links the passion of Christ with sexual passion in ordinary people. The way the *F* in the Fidji logo is designed also vaguely suggests a crucifix.

The infinity sign formed by the body of the snake. Part of the way the snake loops around on the woman's shoulder appears to form the symbol for infinity—perhaps an indication of the infinite nature of the passion that will be generated by wearing Fidji?

The painted fingernails. There is something incongruous, one might think, about a "natural" woman, in Polynesia, wearing painted red fingernails. Maybe the subtext of this advertisement is that you can have the best of both worlds—modernity, sophistication (the perfume is French and therefore, in the popular mind, sophisticated), and elegance as well as the kind of guilelessness and passion we associate with the

TABLE 7.1 Polar Oppositions Drawn From the Fidji Advertisement

Woman of Color (Polynesian)	*White Woman*
nature	urban society
escape	imprisonment
paradise	hell
dark hair	light hair
free sexuality	inhibited sexuality
magic	rationality
Fidji perfume	other perfumes

innocent and natural woman. This duality is, in fact, at the core of the advertisement: a natural woman holding a bottle of French perfume. The bottle mediates between the primitive woman "within a woman" and the average woman's socialized, enculturated, everyday life.

A PARADIGMATIC ANALYSIS OF THE FIDJI ADVERTISEMENT

One of the most famous statements Saussure (1966) ever made explains how people find meaning in their experiences: "Concepts are purely differential and defined not by their positive content but negatively buy their relations with other terms of the system" (p. 117). He adds, "The most precise characteristic [of these concepts] is being what the others are not" (p. 117). In essence, it is the way language works, by forcing us to see differences, that explains how we make sense of things. Meaning is relational, not based on the essences of things themselves.

The French anthropologist Claude Lévi-Strauss (1967) developed a method of analyzing myths that involves finding oppositions in them. In this section I adapt this method of analysis, paradigmatic analysis, to an examination of the Fidji advertisement. Let's look at some of the oppositions generated by the Fidji ad, which suggest what it is not (see Table 7.1). My thesis is that when people look at the ad, they go through the process of generating such oppositions—if they are to find meaning in it.

I am not suggesting that people consciously make a paradigmatic analysis when they see the Fidji ad (or any other advertisement), but if Saussure is correct, and concepts have meaning differentially, they must do something like this on an unconscious level if the advertisement is to make sense to them. The oppositions are, then, implicit in the advertisement.

There is also a good deal of redundancy in the Fidji advertisement, to help get the message across. We see the word *Fidji* three times—in the caption, on the bottle, and in the copy in the upper right-hand part of the ad. Further, the image of the woman with a flower in her hair (like the women in Gauguin's paintings) and the snake reinforce the Fidji-paradise theme. The perfume promises magic—to transport women back to earlier times, before life was so complex, and their lives were so full of everyday bothers—back to when, so we imagine, sexuality was natural and uninhibited. The fact that this primitive maiden is holding a bottle of very expensive French perfume is an irony that, no doubt, is lost on most of those to whom the advertisement is directed.

PSYCHOANALYTIC ASPECTS
OF THE FIDJI TEXT

In the semiotic analysis above I have already covered a number of the psychoanalytic aspects of this text, such as the matter of the snake as a phallic symbol. As Freud writes in *The Interpretation of Dreams* (1900/1965), "Many of the beasts which are used as genital symbols in mythology and folklore play the same part in dreams: e.g. fishes, snails, cats, mice (on account of the pubic hair), and above all those most important symbols of the male organ, snakes" (p. 392). This symbolization, he adds, is found not only in dreams, but in other areas as well:

> Symbolism is not peculiar to dreams, but is characteristic of unconscious ideation, in particular among the people, and it is to be found in folklore, and in popular myths, legends, linguistic idioms, proverbial wisdom and current jokes, to a more complete extent than in dreams. (p. 386)

So we are always being affected by symbols—in waking life as well as in dreams. These symbols are, from Freud's point of view, disguised manifestations of latent or unconscious thoughts and desires.

Erich Fromm (1957), as I have noted in Chapter 3, reminds us that for Freud these symbols represent either males and females by their shape or their functions. Flowers and bottles, according to Freud, obviously represent women, so the Fidji advertisement has very female symbols to go along with that preeminent phallic symbol, the snake.

Thus it can be argued that the Fidji ad, through its basic symbolization—the snake, the bottle, and the flower—generates very strong sexual fantasies. Attached to these fantasies are the notions we have about paradise, the tropics, innocent passion, and so on, stemming from what we know about Gauguin's life and our exposure to various novels about life in Polynesia.

There is, for many people, an element of anxiety and fear connected with snakes. Among women, this may be tied to unconscious anxieties and ambivalent feelings they have about men's genitals "penetrating" them. Erik Erikson (1968) has suggested, on the basis of watching children play, that women represent an "incorporative" modality and men a "penetrating" modality. (To sum up Erikson's observations in greatly abbreviated manner: The little girls he watched created enclosures, whereas the little boys built towers.) We also find this penetrating/incorporative polarity in electric plugs and outlets, and in other tools and hardware.

AN ASIDE ON MOISTURIZERS AND ANXIETY

Moisturizers also mine the anxieties many women have about their sexuality and fecundity. A considerable amount of cosmetic advertising emphasizes wetness and moisture, generating anxiety in women that their bodies are continually in danger of becoming dry, arid, and desertlike—that is, devoid of life, infertile, and uninteresting. These ads work to generate anxiety in women about losing their body fluids, which is tied to anxieties they may have about being unable to reproduce or getting older. This, in turn, is connected to matters such as sexuality and desirability. Advertisements for moisturizers create fears that the body is continually "gushing water" and is in danger of

becoming a kind of wasteland, a desert. Dehydration becomes a metaphor for loss of sexual attractiveness and capacity—that is, desexualization.

An advertisement that appeared in *Vogue* some years ago, for a
product called Living Proof Cream Hydracel by Geminesse, explained:

> Water keeps a rose fresh and beautiful. A peach juicy. All living things
> living. The millions of cells in your skin contain water. This water
> pillows and cushions your skin, making it soft and young-looking. But
> for a lot of reasons, cells become unable to hold enough water. And
> the water escapes from your skin. (If you'll forgive us, think of a prune
> drying up and you'll know the whole story.)

Thus a little drama is created and a very powerful metaphor is generated. Advertisements say to women, in effect, "You, who were once
young and sweet and juicy, like a plum, face the danger of becoming
old and drying up and ending up like a prune, if you don't use our
product to moisturize yourself and thus protect yourself."

FINAL COMMENTS ON PERFUME AND ANXIETY

The other side of the anxiety generated by the snake is that without
some kind of magic, a woman will not be able to attract a man, and thus
she really needs to use Fidji if she is to have a rich and satisfying sexual
life. Perfume advertisements are, deep down, about magic and the
fantasy that the power of a particular smell (made of flowers, let us
remember) will excite a man and thus lead to some desired form of
sexual consummation.

Magic, according to Freud, is based ultimately on the omnipotence
of thought. And what is equally interesting is the way magical thinking
switches from the motives or goals of a magical act to the means of
carrying out the magic. Thinking makes it so, but having magic agents,
such as perfume in this case, helps.

We know that aromas do affect us in rather profound ways, so it is
not too far-fetched to suggest that certain scents may have the ability to
excite people sexually. What may add to the mix is the advertising that
makes this argument, over and over again, and associates certain smells

with mass-mediated fantasies found in advertisements and commercials.

Perfumes may work, to a considerable degree, on the basis of a "placebo effect." Wearing perfume may convince a woman that she is sexually alluring, and this confidence may be what is important, not the particular smell (Fidji, Chanel No. 5, Woolworth's best). Could it be that one thing that perfume can do is either mask the "flop sweat" of women who are anxious about whether some man will find them attractive or prevent it by giving them enhanced confidence in themselves? (It is interesting that in most cases the bottles that perfumes come in cost more to make than the perfumes themselves.)

There is something curiously peaceful about the Fidji maiden in paradise with the snake around her shoulders. Her face doesn't reflect any anxiety about the snake, and she holds her bottle of Fidji in her fingers, awkwardly, with a sense of security about herself. Presumably she is wearing Fidji, and thus she need not fear that she will lack companionship. Could it be that Fidji perfume (and all perfumes) is, in mysterious and magical ways, like snake venom—a powerful agent that has an incredible effect upon those on whom it is used? But what does this say about women who use perfumes?

STUDY QUESTIONS AND TOPICS FOR DISCUSSION

1. What aesthetic considerations should be kept in mind by the analyst examining advertisements?
2. How is semiotics useful for interpretation of the Fidji advertisement featured in this chapter?
3. Discuss the various signemes in the Fidji advertisement.
4. What is the secret significance of moisturizers?
5. What role does figurative language play in advertising? Consider the role of metaphor in the Geminesse moisturizer ad mentioned in this chapter.

In this chapter, all-news radio stations are subjected to a Marxist interpretation. These stations are seen as signifiers of a malaise in American culture, and the dependency that people have on these stations is linked to the American capitalist economic system, which generates anxiety and thus a need for constant surveillance. The information hunger many people feel is reinforced by the trivial, often commercial, news presented. A discussion of radio commercials is also offered; these commercials occupy approximately one-third of each broadcasting hour and often create anxiety and many other negative feelings. The chapter ends with an examination of the audiences of radio talk shows and all-news stations, with some speculation about what the demographic figures imply.

CHAPTER 8

All-News Radio and the American Bourgeoisie

hat are we to make of the various all-news radio stations that are now operating in many of the major radio markets in the United States? How can we explain the existence of stations that broadcast news 24 hours a day? One would imagine that all this news would result in incredible overkill or supersaturation; yet the fact is that in many large cities, all-news stations are quite profitable.

The programming at all-news radio stations tends to be highly structured and formulaic: Sports news is broadcast at certain times, as are business news, the weather reports, features, commentaries, local news, network news—all have more or less regular time slots, so that listeners who are looking for certain kinds of news can learn when to tune in and get whatever it is they are interested in.

NEWS AND ALIENATION

The existence of all-news radio stations, and now all-news television stations, indicates that there is a pervasive "information hunger" that this kind of programming helps to assuage. But why this voracity for news? Why this need to keep on top of everything? It is a sign (or, to be more precise, semiotically speaking, a signifier) of a widespread and powerful affliction in American culture—an overpowering sense of anxiety and fear (the signified) that tears at the psyches of many people. It also represents a desire to "participate" in history somehow, even if only vicariously.

Psychoanalysis would describe something like this as a neurosis, a form of behavior that is compulsive, even though it seems quite innocuous (and, perhaps, is even virtuous, given that citizens are supposed to be well informed), but that is fueled by relentless and powerful urges that quite likely are harmful. In extreme cases we may even suggest that "newsaholics" are people who know everything but do nothing—except listen to (or watch) the news. There may even be something of a desire to be like God in these people—all-knowing, all-pervasive—except that the newsaholic is driven not by a sense of being all-powerful, but by the reverse.

Ultimately, it would seem, the anxiety of the heavy news listener is the product of a sense of powerlessness and insignificance, which leads to a need for constant surveillance. From the Marxist perspective, this is quite understandable. Bourgeois capitalist societies generate alienation and a host of afflictions that are connected to it—a sense of powerlessness, insecurity, estrangement, rootlessness, and lack of identity. Because we have no coherent sense of history or ideology, and because we live in a society that may be described as dog-eat-dog, we must, if we are to survive, keep on top of things and never be caught napping.

Our capacity to absorb the enormous amounts of programming aired by all-news stations is tied to this anxiety and to something else (to continue the Marxist critique): What we are offered is not really news but essentially trivia—sensational "junk food for the mind" that does not deal seriously with our social and political problems but instead diverts and entertains us. Because this so-called news is so insubstantial, we are able to devour huge quantities of it and never get full. We lack a well-defined and coherent political sensibility that would enable us to make sense of events. All we get, for the most part, is "figure" divorced from "ground"—that is, a succession of reports on all kinds of things (fires, crimes, political events, film reviews, food tips, the weather) that all occupy the foreground.

This "news" is all superficially interesting and satisfies our curiosity, but it doesn't help us to orient ourselves, because nothing fits together with anything else. The pressure within the news media to cover events as they happen, to get the news first, prevents them from providing useful background information and thoughtful analysis. "To the blind, all things are sudden," someone once said, and to those with no sense of history and social relations, with no understanding of the causes of events and their implications, all-news stations are literally sensational. What we get may be fascinating, but it is not particularly edifying or useful to listeners who wish to uncover the meanings of events.

Frequently, media scholars distinguish between "hard" and "soft" news. Hard news is supposedly serious; it deals with important events in the social, political, and economic arenas. But many of the stories classified as hard news are really the products of the public relations mills of political leaders, government agencies, businesses, and other organizations. News reporters are, as a rule, highly moral and responsible professionals who do the best they can to avoid being manipulated, to offer accurate information, and so forth, but they have, without recognizing it, adopted the establishment's point of view, and their ideas are, as Marxists would put it, "the ideas of the ruling class."

NEWS AND RULING-CLASS IDEOLOGY

A study of televised news conducted in Great Britain reached some conclusions about the role of broadcasters in the presentation of ideology:

> News talk occurs within a cultural framework which stresses balance and impartiality. Yet despite this, detailed analysis reveals that it consistently maintains and supports a cultural framework within which viewpoints favourable to the *status quo* are given *preferred* and *privileged* readings.
>
> This representation of events as news is not governed by a conscious attempt to present ideology. The journalists and producers and those they allow to broadcast of course believe that their routines and codes merely serve to fashion the news into intelligible and meaningful bulletins. (Glasgow University Media Group, 1980, p. 122)

The ideological assumptions made by newscasters are not generally recognized, either by them or by their audiences, and this makes them all the more insidious. News professionals select items to focus attention on from a huge inventory of what is available. Their selection of items for broadcast (along with their failure to provide audiences with background on those items) is crucial. What is neglected? What is not seen as worth dealing with? What is determined to have little news value? These are some questions we might ask as we consider the adequacy of the news diet available on all-news radio stations. It is possible that some stories that might be of considerable significance are neglected or mentioned only in passing because of the unconscious assumptions of the news editors and audiences of these news programs, who have been taught over a number of years what is important and what isn't. Some issues, by their nature, are harder than others to uncover or more complicated to analyze; they are often passed over by editors and reporters who face the pressures of limited time and money.

When we get to soft news—features of various kinds—we find an insidious commercialization present, for they almost always contain, as an end result, the promotion of some product or service. We learn about "undiscovered" restaurants, interesting films, and the best boutiques in which to buy this or that kind of clothing. Ultimately, though these features may seem quite innocent, they serve as free advertisements for businesses. From a sociological perspective, the manifest functions of such features are to entertain and to provide useful information; the latent function is to "sell" restaurants, movies, and all manner of other things. To the Marxist, hard news and soft news are more or less the same; both help to support the ideological perspectives of the ruling classes and fuel the engines of consumption.

COMMERCIALS AND ANXIETY

The most important engines of consumption in radio broadcasting are the commercials; about 16 to 18 minutes of every hour—roughly one-third of broadcast time—is devoted to commercials. Thus one-third of the information broadcast on all-news stations is product news. When soft news is added to the mix, it is clear that a very large block of news airtime is actually given to commercial information. In addition, most of the imagination, intelligence, and creativity found on radio— and in popular culture in general—is lavished on commercials. This is because they are what is most important; they are the raison d'être for the stations, which, after all, are businesses that exist to make money through the use of the public airwaves.

We are bombarded with slogans, jingles, and announcements that use whatever subliminal or other persuasive techniques are available to make us feel anxious about ourselves, to generate feelings of relative deprivation, and to get us to *buy* something (see Chapter 7 for more on the power of advertising). Ironically, to assuage our bad feelings, to rid ourselves of these anxieties about ourselves and our situations, we turn to the mass media—movies, soap operas, music, even all-news radio stations—which reinforce the very problems we hope they will help us solve. Thus we become caught in a vicious cycle from which there is no escape. The more we listen to the news (and the ubiquitous commercials), the unhappier we get, and the unhappier we get, the more we listen to the news.

When we listen to all-news radio stations, especially for long periods of time, we seldom can avoid ending up disturbed. We become anxious about the world and plagued by various negative emotions. This may explain why, in certain circumstances, no news is good news. Small wonder that the average person listens to all-news stations in only 20- or 30-minute segments.

CAUGHT IN THE MIDDLE

Demographic studies of the audiences of all-news programs indicate that listeners tend to be upscale—that is, affluent professional types who are well educated and, it would seem, far removed from the pathetic figures I have described. Trendy affluents most certainly are not tense, anxiety-ridden souls endlessly searching for security and desperate about keeping abreast of things lest they be caught unawares. Or are they?

Do all of these upscale people have a real sense of security and a well-defined identity? Or is there, perhaps, a faint tinge of desperation showing in the way they follow the business news or listen to the features to be told the "right" movies, the "right" restaurants, and the "right" opinions to have about all kinds of things?

News listeners tend to be middle-class people. Those in the proletariat (who live in poverty) have relatively little interest in the news. These people tend to be fatalists who are unable to change the system that oppresses them; they are generally uninvolved in and unconcerned (except in cases immediate to their interests) about events in the world. Those in the upper classes own the means of production—including the media—and need not worry too much about what is going on. They control the events. Older people also don't worry much about what is going on in the world (aside from issues dealing with social security and related matters) and, instead, listen to talk shows in large numbers. Approximately half of the audience of radio talk shows is composed of people over 65 years old. Young people are busy listening to music stations and worrying about such age-related problems as acne, sex, fashion, cars, and love. When we shear off the relatively old, the very young, the poor, and the rich, we are left with the middle-aged (and postteenage and pre-middle-aged), middle-class people who are the prime customers of all-news programs.

The members of this group have the most to gain or to lose from the tide of events. They have no power to alter the system set up by the upper classes—nor do they have the desire to. They have been thoroughly indoctrinated by the ideology fed them day and night on their radios and through the other media and hope only to improve their situation so that someday they may join the upper class they have tried so long to emulate. But this requires constant attention to the news if they are to maintain their current status and possibly someday get the edge on their competitors—other middle-class people much like themselves. These people, according to Marxist thinking, are the guilt-ridden victims of all-news radio.

STUDY QUESTIONS AND
TOPICS FOR DISCUSSION

1. What is the relationship between news (and information hunger) and alienation? How is sensationalism in the news related to this alienation?
2. How are news programs and the ideology they reflect interpreted from a Marxist viewpoint?

3. Define *relative deprivation* and explain how it is related to a Marxist interpretation of radio programming.
4. Why are middle-class Americans so passionately "involved" with news?

Epilogue

Shmoos and Analysis

A number of years ago, when I was about to enter graduate school to work on a doctorate in American studies, my brother, Jason, suggested I not bother. "American studies is like a Shmoo," he said. (For those who don't know what Shmoos are, let me explain. They are mythical creatures that love more than anything else to do things for people, including offering themselves as food. Fried, they taste like steak; baked, like ham; roasted, like roast beef. Their whiskers can be used for toothpicks and their skin for leather. And they multiply like crazy. They are the invention of Al Capp, and they appeared in *Li'l Abner*—one of the most important comic strips ever produced in the United States.)

"American studies is like a Shmoo. If you bake it you're a historian, if you fry it you're a literary critic, if you boil it you're a sociologist, if you broil it you're a political scientist."

We can apply this insight to analysis, for critics and media analysts don't just exist, they always have a point of view (or, with eclectic analysts, several points of view). And they bring their point (or points) of view, their sense of the world, their understanding of people and society to whatever it is they analyze. Analysis, at least as I see things, doesn't just exist in and of itself.

For this volume I have selected four techniques that I consider to be of great importance, but there are other techniques I could have addressed. The room in which our four critics sat watching that episode of *Dallas* could have been crowded with people. There might have been a literary critic, who would have been concerned with such matters as plot, theme, point of view, motivation of characters, setting, and tone.

There might have been a "myth-ritual-symbol" critic, with an anthropological background, with what might be described as "culturological" interests. An ethical critic might have focused on moral problems raised in the episode and other philosophical concerns, whereas an aesthetically oriented critic might have been concerned with aspects of the production such as lighting, camera angles, kinds of shots, fades, cutting, and sound effects. Jungian critics would look for archetypes, shadows, anima and animus figures, heroes, trickster figures, and so on. Experts in nonverbal behavior might examine the program in terms of the facial expressions of the characters (especially in close-ups), their body language, and a host of similar concepts.

The goal of media analysis, as I see it, is to offer the most comprehensive, most interesting, most profound reading of a text possible. Some people think that analysis is a waste of time and that it "destroys" a work. This is a "know-nothing" position that assumes that the more mindless our responses to television programs, films, or whatever, the better off we are.

I would argue that we need analysis if we are to appreciate and understand a work fully. Furthermore, creative artists of all kinds (and in all media) need to be self-critical—in the positive sense of the term—so that they can understand how they generated the effects they were after, what worked and what didn't. You need theory in order to be able to practice successfully and effectively; otherwise the successes you have are just the results of accidents and luck. Just as creative people are generally also very analytic, analysts are often also very creative. I hope that this volume has provided some encouragement for others to combine analysis and creativity.

STUDY QUESTIONS AND TOPICS FOR DISCUSSION

1. How are media criticism, analysis, interpretation, and so on like a Shmoo?
2. What techniques for analysis other than those addressed in this book might be applied to works of art?
3. Is there an ideal way of analyzing works of art? If so, what is it?

4. When semioticians, psychoanalysts, Marxists, and sociologists analyze a given text and come up with different interpretations, who is
   right? Or is there no such thing as a "right" interpretation of a text?
5. Analyze a particular text (a film, a television show, a book, or
   something else) assigned by your instructor from the four points of
   view discussed in this volume. Which approach do you find most
   useful and interesting? Why?

Appendix

*Simulations, Activities,
Games, and Exercises*

I have developed a number of simulations, activities, games, and exercises (which I refer to collectively as *learning games*) that involve applying various aspects of media analysis techniques to the popular arts and the mass media. These learning games require players to move from the level of theory, where the concepts may be vague (and their utility not terribly clear), to that of practice, where they can see how the concepts and theories associated with the four methodologies discussed in the book can help them make sense of works of popular culture as well as create them.

Generally speaking, when I have the students in my courses play such learning games, I divide the class into groups of three or four; all students in each group are required to participate in the activities, but I ask each group to select one member to function as the designated "scribe" (to do the actual writing). Many of these learning games also make suitable homework assignments, for individuals or for teams of players. However, it should be kept in mind that the emphasis in these learning games is on "play"; I've found that my students find them both enjoyable and valuable. In games that involve scripts or stories, team members can take on the roles to act out what they've written. In other kinds of games, the "findings" of the various teams can serve as the basis of classroom discussion. Depending on the classroom, the class, and the context, variations on all of these learning games can be devised, of course, and new games can be created. Several of the learning games presented below are adapted from my book *Narratives in Popular Culture, Media, and Everyday Life* (1997).

ANATOMY OF A TALE

In my discussion of Vladimir Propp's *Morphology of the Folktale* (1928/1968) in Chapter 1, I have shown how Propp's functions can be used to analyze a story. In this exercise, you are to write a story based on the set of Propp's functions listed below. To play this game, you should use the descriptions of the functions listed below in writing your story. Remember that you can modernize things—thus, at the end, the hero need not literally marry a princess and ascend the throne.

Remember, when you write your story, to (a) use the past tense, (b) include description and dialogue, and (c) make sure there's action and conflict, to keep interest. (Do *not* write a fairy tale in this exercise.) Base your story on the following functions:

1. *Initial situation:*   Members of family, hero introduced.
2. *Absentation:*   One of the members of the family absents him- or herself.
3. *Interdiction:*   Interdiction addressed to hero (can be reversed).
4. *Violation:*   Interdiction is violated.
5. *Villainy:*   Villain causes harm to member of the family.
6. *Mediation:*   Misfortune made known, hero is dispatched.
7. *Receipt of agent:*   Hero acquires use of magical agent.
8. *Spatial change:*   Hero led to object of his search.
9. *Struggle:*   Hero and villain join in combat.
10. *Branding:*   Hero is branded.
11. *Victory:*   Villain is defeated.
12. *Unfounded claims:*   False hero is exposed.
13. *Wedding:*   Hero is married, ascends the throne.

After the stories are written, teams or individuals should share their stories so that the larger group can see how different stories can be even when they use the same Proppian functions.

PARADIGMATIC ANALYSIS

Lévi-Strauss (1967) has argued that the paradigmatic analysis of a text tells us what it "really" means, in contrast to a syntagmatic (Proppian) analysis of a text, which focuses on what happens. In this modification of Lévi-Strauss's methods, you will be looking for various paired oppositions that give a text meaning. Saussure (1966) has suggested that concepts are defined differentially; the same applies to characters in texts, their actions, and so on.

A *Lévi-Straussian Analysis of* Upstairs, Downstairs

Upstairs, Downstairs is a television series that deals with the lives of all the people in a wealthy English household: the wealthy family (the Bellamys) and all their servants. The title offers the basic opposition, but even if the series had been called something else, we would have found this opposition to be central.

Upstairs	*Downstairs*
masters who command	servants who obey
wealthy	poor
leisure	hard work
marriage and infidelity	bachelorhood/spinsterhood

The above list applies to the series in general, but similar lists could be generated for specific episodes in the series, showing sets of oppositions based on the events that take place within those episodes. From this very simple set of polar oppositions, it is clear what the core of the series is.

Lévi-Strauss was interested in myth and not popular culture per se, but his ideas can be adapted to help us understand many kinds of texts, such as spy stories, detective stories, and science fiction tales.

Steps in Playing Lévi-Strauss

1. To take part in this activity, you need a narrative text, one that tells a story. You may choose a film or an episode from a television series to analyze, or your instructor may give you a story to work with, such as the following:

   In the beginning God created the heaven and the earth. And the earth was without form, and void; and darkness was upon the face of the deep. And the Spirit of God moved upon the face of the waters. And God said, "Let there be light": and there was light. And God saw the light, that it was good: and God divided the light from the darkness. And God call the light Day, and the darkness he called Night. And the evening and the morning were the first day.

2. Decide what you believe are the two opposing concepts that are central to the text you are analyzing, concepts that will enable you to deal with the various characters and most important events in the text. Make sure that you find real oppositions as opposed to simple negations (for example, unhappy is not the opposite of happy).

3. Create a list of oppositions based on your text like the one above for *Upstairs, Downstairs*. Remember that the terms on both sides should be linked to specific events in the story.

It should be noted that this process of finding oppositions is not done consciously by most people who read novels, see teleplays, or go to the movies. But if Lévi-Strauss and Saussure are right, we have to elicit such oppositions in order to understand any story. We are so adept at doing this, and we do it so quickly, that we are not conscious of what we are doing.

DREAM ANALYSIS

According to psychoanalytic theory (and most psychologists would agree), dreams play a very significant role in our lives. Freud used his theories about symbolization, condensation, displacement, and so on to analyze dreams, as noted in Chapter 3. Now I offer a dream taken from Freud's (1900/1965) book on dreams and ask you to decode it, as best you can, using the concepts discussed in Chapter 3.

I went into a kitchen in search of some pudding. Three women were standing in it; one of them was the hostess of the inn and was twisting something about in her hands, as though she was making Knodel [dumplings]. She answered that I must wait until she was ready. I felt impatient and went off with a sense of injury. I put on an overcoat. But the first I tried on was too long for me. I took it off, rather surprised to find it was trimmed with fur. A second one that I put on had a long strip with a Turkish design let into it. A stranger with a long face and a short pointed beard came up and tried to prevent my putting it on, saying it was his. I showed him then that it was embroidered all over with a Turkish pattern. He asked: "What have the Turkish (designs, stripes . . .) to do with you?" But we then became quite friendly with each other.

What sense can you make of the events that take place in this dream? In addition to analyzing this dream, you may wish to write down a dream you've had and try to analyze it.

WRITING A THERAPEUTIC FAIRY TALE

This exercise stems from the brief discussion in Chapter 3 concerning Bruno Bettelheim's book *The Uses of Enchantment* (1977). Bettelheim recounts how traditional Hindu healers often compose individualized fairy tales for their patients to help them deal with their problems. The patients study the fairy tales and learn, by identifying with the characters, something about their problems and how to solve them.

In this exercise, pretend that you are a Hindu healer and are writing a fairy tale to help a person deal with an assortment of psychological afflictions. Please do the following:

Write a traditional (not a modernized parody) fairy tale that starts "Once upon a time, long, long ago" and concludes "and so they all lived happily ever after." Use dialogue, description, conflict, and action.

Write in the past tense, and include typical characters from fairy tales: kings, queen, princes and princesses, dragons, animal helpers, heroes with names like "Jack" or "Tom."

Have the actions of the characters reflect and provide resolutions for the numerous psychological problems of the person who has been assigned to you from the following choices:

Person 1: Oedipus complex, castration anxiety, regression

Person 2: penis envy, narcissism, rationalization

Person 3: anal eroticism, ambivalence, fixation

Person 4: Oedipus complex, narcissism, fixation

Person 5: fixation, castration anxiety, narcissism

Person 6: Oedipus complex, ambivalence, sibling rivalry

ORIGIN TALES

Every comic book hero or heroine, or team of heroes and heroines, has an origin tale—a page or two in which the character is introduced to the audience. The most famous of these, no doubt, is the one for Superman, which tells of his origins on Krypton, his long travel in a spaceship to the planet Earth, his being found by the kindly couple who adopted him (the Kents), his great powers, and so on.

In this activity, you are to draw an origin tale for a superhero or superheroine you have created. Draw your tale in 10 or 12 frames on a piece of paper or cardboard that is a standard size agreed to by all of the teams or individuals participating in this activity. Remember to observe the following rules:

- ✔ Use 10 or 12 frames. Make real drawings and color them in. Do not use stick figures.
- ✔ Have the characters speak in balloons. You can also use parts of panels to give continuity information.
- ✔ Pay attention to facial expressions, characters' clothing, action depictions, sound effects, and dialogue.
- ✔ Consider what special abilities, powers, and so on your hero or heroine has.
- ✔ Tell a story. Even though you are introducing your character to an audience, you still have to include action, conflict, and so on.

When completed, the origin tales of all participants should be exhibited together so that everyone can observe the different kinds of heroes, heroines, villains, monsters, and so on that have been created. Are there any similarities among the various figures or among the themes dealt with? What do the origin tales reflect about the age group of those creating the tales and about American culture and society?

RADIO SCRIPTS

In this exercise, you are to write a radio script that dramatizes and somehow explains semiotic analysis, psychoanalytic theory, Marxist criticism, or sociological analysis (or some combination of these techniques, or all of them) to a person who has not studied these techniques. Use some well-known film or television show for your subject, and follow these rules to create a script that appears in radio's traditional format:

- ✓ Divide the page into two columns. In the left-hand column, which should be about 1½ inches wide, use ALL CAPS for the names of the characters and indications for MUSIC or SFX (sound effects).
- ✓ Place instructions concerning music or sound effects, in ALL CAPS and underlined (or italicized), in the right-hand column.
- ✓ Use the right-hand column for the dialogue, always in Caps and Lowercase (that is, in usual sentence style). (Having only the dialogue in caps and lowercase makes it easy to differentiate dialogue from other aspects of the script.)
- ✓ Place instructions about how a character is to read his or her lines (or other action a character is to take) in ALL CAPS and in parentheses before or following the affected dialogue. Always double space dialogue.

SFX	*BAR SOUNDS: PEOPLE TALKING, LAUGHTER, ETC.*
JOHN	(ANGRILY) You stood me up last night. And this wasn't the first time.
GWEN	(COYLY) Please forgive me, John. I was so involved learning about media criticism that I lost track of time.
MUSIC	*JUKEBOX PLAYS FRANK SINATRA SINGING "MY WAY"*
JOHN	I'm sorry, Gwen. But it's too late. We're finished.
GWEN	If that's the way you feel, it's fine with me. Besides, I was just in the middle of the section on dreams in the psychoanalytic chapter. Last night I dreamed you were a frog. What can that mean?

TELEVISION NARRATIVE ANALYSIS

In this exercise, you will examine a television narrative in terms of some of the methods and concepts discussed in this book. After viewing the assigned television show, do the following:

✔ Apply Propp's morphology to the text. Try to find six or eight of Propp's functions that are reflected in the television program. List all functions and describe the events in the text that exemplify each function.

✔ Make a paradigmatic analysis of the text; that is, list a series of paired oppositions that you find in the text. All the terms on the left side should relate to one another and be opposite to all the terms on the right side of your list.

✔ Think of the text as being a kind of "public" dream. Analyze the text in terms of the symbolic significance of the major events in the text. What might they reflect about the psyche, politics, society, culture?

You should be able to justify your choices and be prepared to explain why you did what you did in all three cases. If there are widespread disagreements about the application of Propp to the text, the oppositions found in the text, and/or the analysis of the symbolism in the text, what does that mean?

THE PROPP GAME

The power of signs (in particular, signifiers) to generate meanings, feelings, attitudes, and so on is of great use to those who create the products of the mass media, for it is precisely the ability to stimulate particular feelings at specific moments that enables directors, actors, and others to reach people with their media texts.

The secret is to work backwards—that is, start by deciding what effect you want and then figure out how to create it or generate it using the various aspects of the medium at your disposal. In television, for instance, certain effects are created through the use of color, camera angles and shots, sound effects, music, dialogue, and action. All television viewers learn how to interpret the various signs they see and hear—they become "television literate," which means they know how to read the codes and conventions used in TV.

In this game you will start with an effect (or concept) and work backwards to figure out how to create it, but this will take a simplified form. Here is how the game is played:

1. Choose (or your instructor will assign) a signified or—for our purposes, a concept or idea (good examples would be *love*, *hate*, *genius*).

Love	Hate	Horror	Terror
Los Angeles	Frenchness	Genius	The Future
Power	Alienation	Loneliness	Secret Agent
Wisdom	Stupidity	Happiness	Sadness

Figure A.1. Chart for the Propp Game

2. List a number of signifiers that can be used to signify the concept desired. All your signifiers must be visual images—objects, tangible things.
3. List as many signifiers as you can. (In some cases, the gestalt or collection of objects will help establish the precise meaning desired.)
4. Be certain that the objects and artifacts you use do not mislead people, making them think of the wrong signified.

An Example

Suppose your signified is "secret agent." You are a director and want to indicate to your viewers that secret agents are part of your story. Some of the signifiers you might use if your secret agents include trench coats, dark sunglasses, slouch hats, pistols with silencers, and fast sports cars. A six-gun would not be appropriate—it would be misleading.

METAPHORS

A metaphor is traditionally understood as a literary device in which one thing is seen in terms of another. That is, a metaphor suggests some kind of relationship between two things in the form of an analogy. For example, the statement "My love is a red rose" is a metaphor in which a person's love and a red rose are equated. (Simile is a relatively weak form of metaphor that uses *like* or *as*; for example, "My love is like a red rose.")

Metaphors are more than just literary devices, however; they actually affect our thought processes in profound ways. Linguists George Lakoff and Mark Johnson (1980) discuss the role of metaphor in our lives:

> Metaphor is typically viewed as a characteristic of language alone, a matter of words rather than thought or action. For this reason, most people think they can get along perfectly well without metaphor. We have found, on the contrary, that metaphor is pervasive in everyday life, not just in language but in thought and action. Our ordinary conceptual system, in terms of which we both think and act, is fundamentally metaphoric in nature.
>
> The concepts that govern our thought are not just matters of the intellect. They also govern our everyday functioning, down to the most mundane details. Our concepts structure what we perceive, how we get around in the world, and how we relate to other people. Our conceptual system thus plays a central role in defining our everyday realities. (p. 3)

They also point out that metaphors help shape our futures:

> Metaphors may create realities for us, especially social realities. A metaphor may thus be a guide for future action. Such actions will, of course, fit the metaphor. This will, in turn, reinforce the power of the metaphor to make experience coherent. (p. 156)

As Lakoff and Johnson argue, the metaphors we employ have implications for the ways we live; they take on a kind of logical and coercive power.

How to Play the Metaphor Game

Take the following steps:

1. Write down a metaphor.

Love is a game.	Love is a fever.
1. Games end.	1. You're all hot.
2.	2.
3.	3.
4.	4.
5.	5.
6.	6.
7.	7.
8.	8.
9.	9.
10.	10.
11.	11.

Figure A.2. Metaphors to Analyze

2. List the logical implications of your metaphor.
3. Consider whether your metaphor is likely to be beneficial or harmful to a person who accepts it—and its logical implications.
4. Try to improve on your metaphor.

Later, think about some of the metaphors you live by. What are your essential metaphors? What implications do these metaphors have for your life?

Things to Consider

After playing this game, what conclusions do you come to about the ways people find meaning in life?

1. Where do we pick up the metaphors that shape our lives? Be as specific as possible: State a metaphor and see if you can find out where it comes from.

2. Is it possible that what disturbs many people is that they have, unintentionally, internalized destructive (or self-destructive) metaphors?

3. How can we deal with the problems caused by destructive metaphors? Is it also possible that people are illogical and that they don't live by the logical implications of the metaphors they accept? That is, is it possible that Lakoff and Johnson are incorrect about people living by metaphors because people are so "illogical" or "complex"?

Figure A.2 presents two metaphors for you to analyze. Write down as many implications of each metaphor as you can think of. Each list has already been started for you with an example.

ADVERTISING ANALYSIS

In this exercise, you will use one, several, or all of the methodologies you have learned about in this volume (semiotics, psychoanalytic theory, sociological theory, Marxist theory) to analyze advertisements.

First, choose some advertisements that are full of material that lends itself to analysis—preferably ads with people, objects, interesting backgrounds, interesting copy, and so on. Next, apply the methodology or methodologies your instructor assigns you to use to analyze the ads you have collected. (Be sure to review Chapter 7 before undertaking your own analysis.) In analyzing your ads, consider all of the following:

✔ signifiers and signifieds
✔ icons, indexes, and symbols
✔ sociological phenomena: demographics of people in the ads and of the people toward whom the ads are targeted, reflections of socioeconomic classes, lifestyles, and so on
✔ the nature of the appeals made to sell the products, through both the copy and the people used in the ads

- ✔ the designs of the advertisements, including typefaces used, colors, and other aesthetic matters
- ✔ the publications in which you found the ads, and the expected audiences of those publications

PLAYING AARON WILDAVSKY

The work of Aaron Wildavsky offers some ideas that can be used to assess and analyze the media, popular culture, and related areas from an interesting perspective. Wildavsky has drawn upon his work with a British anthropologist, Mary Douglas, to explain and describe the four political cultures found in democratic societies, the members of which he calls hierarchical elitists, competitive individualists, egalitarians, and fatalists (see the discussion of Wildavsky's work in Chapter 3).

Figure A.3 shows some of the traits associated with the members of the four political cultures. In this game, you will be looking for reflections of the four political cultures in films, television programs, books, and so on. The connections you find will not necessarily be overt or recognized by many people who form the audiences for these works (but we know that people seek reinforcement for their beliefs and want to avoid dissonance, so it is logical to assume that people choose texts that are congruent with their beliefs and values).

Take the following steps:

1. Find one or more specific examples of each of the topics listed in Figure A.3. Do not deal with genres; rather, select particular films, television programs, songs, and so on (for example, "God Bless America," not "patriotic song").
2. Make sure your example fits the category (to the extent that this is possible). In some cases, you may have to do a bit of stretching, but try to be as precise as you can.
3. Be prepared to explain and justify your choices.
4. Consider matters such as trends and new developments in doing this exercise.

	Elitists	Individualists	Egalitarians	Fatalists
	leadership from top	individuals are own leaders	charismatic leaders	no concern with leadership
	inequality natural	equality of opportunity	equality of needs basic	inequality natural
	top helps bottom	every person for him- or herself	spread wealth to all	hope for luck
	keep order	make money	make everyone equal	survive
Songs				
TV shows				
Films				
Magazines				
Books				
Heroes				
Heroines				
Games				
Sports				

Figure A.3. The Four Political Cultures and Popular Culture

Glossary

Aberrant decoding: The decoding or interpretation of texts by audiences in ways that differ from the ways the creators of the texts expect them to be decoded. According to semiotician Umberto Eco (1972), aberrant decoding is the rule, rather than the exception, when it comes to the mass media.

Administrative research: Research that focuses on ways of making communication by organizations and other entities more efficient and more effective. Compare with *critical research*, which has more interest in social justice and related considerations.

Aesthetics: In the context of this volume, elements that appeal to the senses; in the case of mass media, these include lighting, sound, music, kinds of camera shots and other camera work, and editing, all of which affect the ways members of audiences react.

Agenda-setting theory: The theory that institutions of mass communication determine not what we think, but what we think about. They set the agenda for our decision making and thus influence our social and political lives.

Alienation: In the context of this volume, estrangement from the self [from *alien*, which means someone with no connections to others—*a* (no) and *lien* (ties)]. According to Marx, alienation is the central problem of bourgeois societies and affects everyone in them; capitalism produces material things, but it also produces alienation.

Allegory: A metaphorical story that has symbolic significance, that has implications beyond the story itself. Allegories employ themes and ideas of a broad philosophical nature and convey some kind of a moral. For example, the television series *The Prisoner* (in which a man is imprisoned on a mysterious island, is deprived of his name and given a number instead, and has various adventures in which he fights with the administration of the island and tries to escape, eventually destroying the island and succeeding) can be seen as an allegory of the triumph of the human spirit and democratic individualism over the forces of a totalitarian bureaucracy and adversity in general.

Ambivalence: A defense mechanism involving a simultaneous feeling of love and hatred or attraction to and repulsion toward the same person or thing.

Anomie: A condition in which people reject the norms of a given society (from the Greek *anomos*, meaning "no norms" or "no law"). The term was made popular by the French sociologist Émile Durkheim.

Audience: In the context of this volume, a collection of individuals who receive a media text—watch a television program, listen to a radio program, attend a film or some kind of artistic performance, and so on. Members of an audience may be together in one room or scattered; in the case of television, each may be watching on his or her own set. In technical terms, members of an audience are addressees who receive mediated texts sent by some addresser.

Base: In Marxist thought, the economic system found in a given society. The base shapes (but does not determine) the superstructure—the institutions found in the society, such as art, religion, the legal system, and the educational system.

Castration anxiety: In Freudian theory, the fear young males have that they will be castrated by their fathers. This anxiety leads young boys to renounce their love for their mothers and to identify with their fathers, and thus overcome their Oedipus complexes.

Characters: The people found in a story whose actions constitute the story and lead to its resolution. Readers must find characters interesting and want to follow their adventures, so authors have to find ways of making their characters worth bothering with. As a rule, the characters in narratives are not representative of ordinary people. On television, for example, there is a far greater percentage of police officers, private detectives, and killers than exist in real life, and a far smaller proportion of blue-collar workers. Many narrative theorists argue that character is the basis of action in narratives, whereas others argue that action reveals character.

Class: A group of people or things that have something in common; in the context of this volume, the term refers primarily to social class or, more literally, socioeconomic class—groups of people who differ in terms of income and lifestyle. Marxist theorists argue that there is a ruling class that shapes the ideas of the proletariat, the working class, and generates "false consciousness" in order to avoid class conflict and revolution.

Class conflict: Conflict between the working class and the ruling class. According to Marxist theory, history is the record of class conflict. This conflict will end when capitalism is replaced by communism and classes are eliminated, because everyone will own the means of production.

Climax or **crisis:** The turning point of a story, when the most important matter is somehow decided, setting the stage for the resolution. A story must have a climax so that it can lead to some kind of resolution that readers find interesting and satisfying.

Codes: Systems of symbols, letters, words, sounds, and so on that generate meaning. Language, for example, is a code. It uses combinations of letters that we call words to mean certain things. The relation between the word and the thing the word stands for is arbitrary, based on convention. In some cases, the term *code* is used to describe hidden meanings and disguised communications.

Cognitive dissonance: The psychological conflict that results within a person when he or she holds clashing beliefs or when his or her actions and beliefs are opposed to each other. According to psychologists, people wish to avoid ideas that challenge the ones they hold, because this creates conflict and other disagreeable feelings. (The term *dissonance* is also used to refer to sounds that clash with one another.)

Content analysis: A nonintrusive methodology in which the researcher examines particular elements in a text or collection of texts to quantify them and use them for statistical analysis.

Critical research: Approaches to media that are essentially ideological, that focus on the social and political dimensions of the mass media and the ways they are used by organizations and others allegedly to maintain the status quo rather than to enhance equality. Compare with *administrative research.*

Cultural homogenization: The destruction of cultures (such as Third World and certain regional cultures) other than the dominant culture, leading to cultural sameness and standardization.

Cultural imperialism or *media imperialism:* The alleged domination of Third World cultures through the transmission of certain values and beliefs via the flow of media products (such as songs, films, and television programs) and popular culture from the United States and a few Western European capitalist countries.

Culture: The specific ideas, arts, customary beliefs, ways of living, behavior patterns, institutions, and values of a group, transmitted from generation to generation. When applied to the arts, the term *culture* is generally used in reference to "elite" kinds of artworks, such as operas, poetry, classical music, and serious novels.

Defense mechanisms: The methods used by the ego to defend itself against pressures from the id, or impulsive elements in the psyche, and superego elements such as conscience and guilt. Some of the more common defense mechanisms are repression (barring unconscious instinctual wishes, memories, and so on from consciousness), regression (returning to earlier stages in one's development), ambivalence (a simultaneous feeling of love and hate toward some person or thing), and rationalization (offering excuses to justify one's actions).

Demographics: Statistical characteristics of people, including race, religion, gender, social class, ethnicity, occupation, place of residence, and age. Compare with *psychographics.*

Deviance: Difference from the norm, whether in values and beliefs or in actions. Attitudes toward various forms of deviance change over time. Many groups that are judged deviant are marginalized—that is, pushed to the margins of society, where they can be ignored or persecuted (or both).

Dysfunctional: Contributing to the breakdown or destabilization of an entity.

Ego: According to Freudian theory, the executant of the id and a mediator between the id and the superego. The ego is involved with the perception of reality and the adaptation to reality.

Emotive function: The function of expression of feelings. According to Jakobson (1988), this is one of the functions of messages; the other functions are referential and poetic.

Ethical criticism: Criticism that is concerned with the moral aspects of what happens in texts and the texts' possible impacts. There is considerable debate about what is ethical in the production of texts and the role ethics should play in the arts and the media.

False consciousness: In Marxist thought, the mistaken ideas that people have about their class, status, and economic possibilities. These ideas help maintain the status quo and are of great use to the ruling class, which wants to avoid changes in the social structure. According to Marx, the ideas of the ruling class are always the ruling ideas in society.

Feminist criticism: Criticism that focuses on the roles of women and how women are portrayed in mass-mediated texts of all kinds. Feminist critics argue that women are typically depicted as sexual objects, as housewives, as weak or helpless or mindless, and so on, and this has negative affects on the socialization of young women and young men, and on society in general.

Formulaic texts: Highly conventional texts with stock characters and recognizable plot structures. Genre texts, such as westerns, science fiction stories, detective stories, and romances are often highly formulaic. They take place in certain locations, have specific kinds of characters who engage in predictable kinds of actions. On a continuum from texts that are highly conventional to texts that are highly inventive, formulaic texts are found very close to the conventional end. Some publishers of romance novels, for example, provide their authors with guidelines that specify such details as the ages heroes and heroines should be, what they should look like, whether or not they can be divorced (and if so, when the divorce had to happen), and whether or not they can have sex before marriage.

Frame: In the context of this volume, a story that provides the means of telling other stories within it. For example, Kurosawa's classic film *Rashomon* employs the frame of a group of men taking shelter from the rain in a temple, where they discuss an incident that has occurred from several conflicting viewpoints; their individual stories are then told in flashback. Such frames are useful for plots that have a serial nature and contain a number of stories, such as *1,001 Arabian Nights*.

Functional: Contributing to the maintenance of a system. A functional institution, for example, contributes to the maintenance of society. Compare with *dysfunctional*.

Functional alternative: Something that functions to take the place of something else. For example, professional football can be seen as a functional alternative to religion.

Gatekeepers: Those with the power to determine who or what gets to pass through a certain point. In the context of this volume, gatekeepers include the editors who determine which stories are used in newspapers and on television and radio news programs. In a broad sense, gatekeepers determine what programs and films we see, what songs we hear, and so on.

Gender: The sexual category of an individual—masculine or feminine—and the behavioral traits connected with each category.

Genre: A type of text characterized by a particular style or formula, such as soap opera, news show, sport program, horror show, or detective story. In French, *genre* means "kind" or "class." (For in-depth discussion of genre texts, see Berger, 1992.)

Hypodermic needle theory: The theory, generally discredited now, that holds that all members of an audience "read" a text the same way and get the same things out of it. The metaphor of a hypodermic needle is a reference to how media are assumed to be injecting all audience members with the same message. This model has been replaced, generally speaking, by the reader response theory.

Hypothesis: An assumption that something is true for the purposes of discussion or argument or further investigation. In a sense, a hypothesis is a guess or supposition that is made as a basis from which to explain some phenomenon.

Id: The element of the psyche that is the representative of a person's drives, according to Freud's theory of the psyche (his "structural hypothesis"). It is also the source of energy, but it lacks direction, and so the superego must harness and control it. In popular thought, the id is connected with impulse and lust—with "I want it all now" kind of behavior.

Ideology: A logically coherent, integrated explanation of social, economic, and political matters that helps establish the goals and direct the actions of some group or political entity. People act (and vote or don't vote) on the basis of their ideologies, even those who have never articulated or given any thought to them. Marxist critics typically seek to expose what they would describe as the ideology hidden in works of popular culture.

Image: In the context of this volume, "a collection of signs and symbols—what we find when we look at a photograph, a film still, a shot of a television screen, a print advertisement, or just about anything" (Berger, 1989, p. 38). An image may be a mental or a physical representation. Images can have powerful emotional effects on people, and some images have historical significance. (For in-depth discussion of image, see Adatto, 1993; Messaris, 1994.)

Intentional fallacy: The idea that it is an error to consider the intention of the artist as an important element in the analysis of that artist's work. In literary and aesthetic theory, this has been the subject of considerable debate; some critics believe that an artist's intention is significant and should be considered, to some degree at least, in the analysis of a text.

Latent functions: Hidden, unrecognized, and unintended functions of some activity, entity, or institution. These are contrasted by social scientists with manifest functions, which are recognized and intended.

Lifestyle: The way people live, including the decisions they make about how to decorate their homes (and where they are located), the kinds of cars they drive, the styles of clothes they wear, the kinds of foods they eat and the restaurants they frequent, where they go for vacations, and so on.

Limited effects (of media): Minor effects of media on society. Some mass communication theorists argue that the influence of the mass media is relatively small in the larger scheme of things. They cite research that shows, for example, that effects from media do not tend to be long lasting.

Manifest functions: Obvious and intended functions of some activity, entity, or institution. These are contrasted by social scientists with latent functions, which are hidden and unintended. For example, the manifest function of a person's going to a political rally is to show support for a candidate; the latent function might be for the person to meet others with similar political views.

Mass: In the context of this volume, a large number of people who form the audience for some communication. There is considerable disagreement about how to understand the mass of people who are reached by mass communication. Some theorists believe the mass is made up of individuals who are heterogeneous, do not know one another, are alienated, and do not have a leader. Others attack these notions as not based on fact or evidence, but on theories that are incorrect.

Mass communication: The transfer of messages, information, texts, and the like from a sender of some kind to a large number of people, a mass audience. This transfer is done through the technologies of the mass media—newspapers, magazines, television programs, films, records, computer networks, CD-ROM, and so on. The sender is often a person in some large media organization, the messages are public, and the audience tends to be large and varied.

Medium: In the context of this volume, a means of delivering messages, information, and texts to audiences—that is, a communication medium. There are different ways of classifying media, one of the most common of which is to divide them into print (newspapers, magazines, books, billboards), electronic (radio, television, computers, CD-ROM), and photographic (photographs, films, videos).

Metaphor: A figure of speech that conveys meaning by analogy. It is important to realize that metaphors are not confined to poetry and literary works; according to some linguists, the fundamental way we make sense of things and find meaning in the world is through metaphors. A simile is a weak form of metaphor that uses either *like* or *as* in making an analogy.

Metonymy: A figure of speech that conveys information by association (for example, using the name Rolls Royce to convey that something is expensive or high quality). Along with metaphor, one of the most important ways people convey information to one another is through metonymy, although we tend not to be aware of how much we use association to get our ideas across. A form of metonymy in which the whole represents a part or vice versa is called *synecdoche* (for example, using "the White House" to mean the presidency).

Mimetic theories of art: Theories, dating from Aristotle's time, based on the notion that art imitates reality.

Model: In the context of this volume, an abstract representation that shows how some phenomenon functions. Theories are typically expressed in language, but models tend to be represented graphically or through statistics or mathematics. McQuail and Windahl (1993) define a model as "a consciously simplified description in graphic form of a piece of reality. A model seeks to show the main elements of any structure or process and the relationships between these elements" (p. 2).

Modern/modernist: Falling within the period approximately from the beginning of the 20th century to the 1960s. Modernist artists rejected narrative structure for simultaneity and montage and explored the paradoxical nature of reality. Important modernists include T. S. Eliot, Franz Kafka, James Joyce, Pablo Picasso, Henri Matisse, and Eugene Ionesco. Modernism was superseded, according to many critics, by postmodernism.

Narrowcast: Disseminate a media text narrowly, by focusing on discrete groups. For example, the medium of radio has many stations that tend to focus on, or narrowcast to, particular kinds of groups. This contrasts with broadcasting, which tries to reach as many people as possible.

Nonfunctional: Neither functional nor dysfunctional. Something that is nonfunctional plays no role in the maintenance or breakdown of the entity in which it is found.

Nonverbal communication: Communication that does not involve words, carried out through body language, facial expressions, styles of dress, hairstyles, and so on. Semiotics can shed light on how nonverbal communication works.

Objective theories of art: Theories based on the notion that art functions to project reality (that of the artist), like a lamp, as opposed to reflecting reality, like a mirror.

Opinion leader: A person whose opinions influence those of others. Opinion leaders play an important role in the two-step flow theory of communication, and the existence of opinion leaders is one of the arguments used to counter the mass society hypothesis.

Phallic symbol: An object that resembles the penis, either in shape or in function. Symbolism is a defense mechanism of the ego that permits hidden or repressed sexual or aggressive thoughts to be expressed in disguised form (for further discussion of this topic, see Freud, 1900/1965).

Phallocentric: Dominated by the masculine point of view. Some critics assert that the ultimate source of this domination, that which shapes our institutions and cultures, is the male phallus. In this theory, which many feminist critics accept, a link is made between male sexuality and male power.

Poetic function: The function of expression through poetic language. According to Jakobson (1988), one of the functions of messages is the use of such literary devices as metaphor and metonymy. Messages also have emotive and referential functions.

Political cultures: Cultures comprising people who are similar in terms of their political values and beliefs and in relation to the group boundaries and rules and prescriptions they observe. Wildavsky (1989) asserts that all democratic societies have four political cultures and that all four are needed to balance one another. He calls the members of the four cultures individualists, hierarchical elitists, egalitarians, and fatalists. For an example of how Wildavsky's theories can be applied to mass media and popular culture, see Berger (1990).

Popular: Literally, "of the people" (from the Latin *popularis*). This term can be defined in may ways, but for purposes of this volume, it generally is used in the sense of appealing to large numbers of people.

Popular culture: The culture of the people, usually understood to include certain kinds of texts that appeal to large numbers of people. Mass communication theorists often identify (or confuse) *popular* with *mass*, and suggest that if something is popular, it must be of poor quality, appealing to the mythical "lowest common denominator." Popular culture is generally held to be the opposite of "elite" culture, which includes arts that require a certain level of sophistication and refinement to appreciate, such as ballet, opera, poetry, and classical music. Many critics now question this popular culture/elite culture polarity.

Postmodern/postmodernist: Falling within the period after the modern era, or from approximately the 1960s to the present. According to a leading theorist on the subject, Jean-François Lyotard (1984), postmodernism is characterized by "incredulity toward metanarratives" (p. xxiv). In other words, the old philosophical belief systems that had helped people order their lives and societies are no longer accepted. This has led to a period in which, more or less, anything goes. Postmodern texts may include irony, parody, and the mixing of genres or styles.

Power: The ability to implement one's wishes as far as policy in some entity is concerned. In the discussion of texts, *power* is often used to describe their ability to have emotional impacts upon people—readers, viewers, or listeners. Critics of recent developments in the mass media have noted that smaller and smaller groups of individuals are controlling more and more media outlets; they fear that this concentration of the power of the media in a few hands will translate into political power.

Pragmatic theories of art: Theories based in the notion that art must do something, must have certain consequences that are held to be desirable. Thus art should teach, indoctrinate, or perform some other function. Marxist theorists generally hold to pragmatic theories of art; they believe that art should help indoctrinate people, generate class solidarity, and be used to fight against capitalist bourgeois societies.

Psychoanalytic theory: A theory based on the notion that the human psyche includes an element that Freud calls the "unconscious" that is ordinarily inaccessible to us (unlike consciousness and the preconscious) and that continually shapes and affects our mental functioning and behavior. Freud also emphasizes matters profoundly affected by unconscious imperatives, such as sexuality and the role of the Oedipus complex in people's lives.

Psychographics: A marketing term used to describe the psychological characteristics of groups of people. Compare with *demographics*.

Public: A group of people, a community. Terms such as *public arts* and *public communication* are sometimes substituted for *popular culture* and *mass communication* to avoid the negative connotations of the words *mass* and *popular*. *Public* is also used in opposition to *private*, as in public acts (those meant to be known to the community) contrasted with private acts (which are not meant to be known to others).

Rationalization: In Freudian thought, a defense mechanism of the ego that creates a justification for some action (or for inaction when an action is expected). Ernest Jones, who introduced the term, used it to describe logical and rational reasons that people give to justify behavior that is really caused by unconscious and irrational determinants.

Reader response theory or **reception theory:** The theory that readers (who include those who read books, watch television programs, go to films, listen to texts on the radio) play an important role in the realization of texts. Texts, then, function as sites for the creation of meaning by readers, and different readers interpret given texts differently. Compare with the *hypodermic needle theory* of media.

Referential function: The function of the expression of relationships between people and/or things. According to Jakobson (1988), the referential function of speech is to help speakers relate to their surroundings. He contrasts this with emotive and poetic functions of speech.

Relativism: In philosophical thought, the belief that truth is relative and not absolute; there are no objective standards. In ethical thought, relativism suggests there are no moral or ethical absolutes. Thus different cultures have different ways of living and practices that are as valid as those of any other culture. That is, morality and ethical behavior are relative to particular groups and cannot be generalized to include all human beings. This contrasts with the notion that there are ethical absolutes or universals that can and should be applied to everyone.

Role: A socialized way of behaving that is appropriate to a particular situation. A person generally plays many roles with different people during a given day: parent, student, worker, and so on.

Sapir-Whorf hypothesis: The hypothesis that language is not something transparent that merely conveys information from one person to another, but rather something that affects the ways people think and act. According to this hypothesis, language is not like a window-pane but more like a prism. This argument is pushed to its extreme by Marshall McLuhan's assertion that "the medium is the message."

Secondary modeling system: The system beyond that of language, our primary modeling system (Lotman, 1977), through which we use language to create art. For example, works of art that use such phenomena as myths and legends function as secondary modeling systems (that is, they are secondary to language).

Selective attention or **selective inattention:** Attention paid only to what we choose. We have a tendency to avoid messages that conflict with our beliefs and values (i.e., that would create cognitive dissonance), and we do this through selective attention. Thus people who belong to a particular political culture (as described by Wildavsky,

1989) tend to search for entertainments that reinforce their values and avoid those that would generate dissonance.

Semiotics: Literally, the science of signs (from the Greek *semeion*, meaning "sign"). A sign is anything that can be used to stand for anything else. According to C. S. Peirce, one of the founders of the science, a sign "is something which stands to somebody for something in some respect or capacity" (quoted in Zeman, 1977, p. 24).

Serial texts: Texts that continue over long periods of time. Examples include comic strips, soap operas, and other television narratives that are on for extended periods of time. Serial texts pose problems for critics of deciding what to consider when analyzing them—the whole of a series or the individual episodes?

Shadow: In Jungian thought, the dark side of the psyche, which we attempt to keep hidden. The shadow contains repressed and unfavorable aspects of our personalities as well as normal instincts and creative impulses. Thus in all of us there is a continual battle between shadow aspects of our personalities and our egos, which also contain some negative features.

Social controls: Ideas, beliefs, values, and mores of a society that shape people's beliefs and behaviors. People are both individuals, with certain distinctive physical and emotional characteristics and desires, and members of societies. They are shaped, to a certain degree, by the institutions—especially education and the media—found in their societies.

Socialization: The processes by which societies teach individuals how to behave: what rules to obey, roles to assume, and values to hold. Socialization has traditionally been a function of the family, educators, clergy, and peers, but the mass media seem to have usurped this function to a considerable degree nowadays, with consequences that are not always positive.

Socioeconomic class: A group categorized according to income and related social status and lifestyle. In Marxist thought, the ruling class shapes the consciousness of the working class; history is, in essence, a record of class conflict.

Stereotypes: Commonly held, simplistic, and often inaccurate group-held portraits of categories of people. Stereotypes can be positive, negative, or mixed, but generally they are negative in nature. Stereo-typing always involves gross overgeneralization.

Subculture: A subgroup within the dominant culture that differs in religion, ethnicity, sexual orientation, beliefs, values, behaviors, life-styles, or in some other way from the dominant culture. Any complex society is likely to have a considerable number of subcultures, and the people in subcultures are often marginalized by the dominant culture.

Superego: The agency in the psyche that is related to conscience and morality. According to Freud, the superego is involved with pro-cesses such as approval and disapproval of wishes on the basis or whether or not they are moral, critical self-observation, and sense of guilt over wrongdoing. The functions of the superego are largely unconscious, and are opposed to the id element in the psyche. Mediating between the two, and trying to balance them, is the ego.

Symbol: Something that stands for something else (from the Greek *symballein*, which means "to put together"). A symbol brings two things together—for example, a particular object and an act by a character that has some higher meaning. In narratives, certain ob-jects, events, or actions by characters have symbolic significance when they refer to things outside of themselves. Thus in *The Maltese Falcon*, the falcon has a symbolic significance, representing the vil-lain's greed and obsessiveness and, by implication, the greed of a number of others—who are willing to lie, cheat, and kill to get their hands on it. The falcon turns out, ironically, to be made of lead, and thus also symbolizes the futility of much human action and the genius individuals have for acting in self-destructive ways. In order to understand symbolism, we have to learn (through socialization and enculturation, for example) what various symbols mean. Critics often distinguish between *allegory* and *symbolism*, using the latter term for something that has a fixed, transcendental significance and the former for something whose meaning becomes evident as the action progresses.

Text: In the context of this volume, any work of art in any medium. The term *text* is used by critics as a convenience, to avoid the need to specify particular kinds of works.

Theory: A systematic and logical attempt, expressed in language, to explain and predict phenomena. Theories differ from concepts, which define phenomena that are being studied, and from models, which are abstract, usually graphic in nature, and explicit about what is being studied.

Trickster figure: In Jungian thought, a figure who represents the earliest period in the development of the hero. Characteristics of the trickster include mischievousness, physical appetites that dominate behavior, desire for the gratification of primary needs, and actions that are often cynical, cruel, and unfeeling.

Two-step flow theory: The theory that mass communication reaches and affects people in a two-step process: First, the media influence opinion leaders; second, the opinion leaders influence others.

Uses and gratifications: A sociological theory that audiences use the mass media (or certain texts or genres of texts) for certain purposes and that they gain certain gratifications from the use of those media. Researchers who subscribe to this theory focus on how audiences use the media, rather than on how the media affect audiences.

Values: Abstract and general beliefs or judgments about what is right and wrong, or good and bad, that have implications for individuals' behavior and for social, cultural, and political entities. From a philosophical point of view, values are the source of several problems. For example, how does one determine which values are correct or good and which are wrong or bad? That is, how do we justify our values? Are values objective or subjective? What happens when groups that hold different central values conflict?

Youth culture: A subculture formed by young people around some area of interest, usually connected with leisure and entertainment, such as rock music or some aspect of computers—games, hacking, and so on. Typically, youth cultures adopt distinctive ways of dressing and develop institutions that cater to their needs. (Frith, 1981, discusses this topic at length.)

References

Adatto, K. (1993). *Picture perfect: The art and artifice of public image making*. New York: Basic Books.

Bakhtin, M. M. (1981). *The dialogic imagination: Four essays* (M. Holquist, Ed.; C. Emerson & M. Holquist, Trans.). Austin: University of Texas Press.

Barthes, R. (1972). *Mythologies*. New York: Hill & Wang.

Berger, A. A. (1976a). *Culture-codes*. Unpublished manuscript.

Berger, A. A. (1976b). *The TV-guided American*. New York: Walker.

Berger, A. A. (1989). *Seeing is believing: An introduction to visual communication*. Mountain View, CA: Mayfield.

Berger, A. A. (Ed.). (1990). *Agitpop: Political culture and communication theory*. New Brunswick, NJ: Transaction.

Berger, A. A. (1992). *Popular culture genres: Theories and texts*. Newbury Park, CA: Sage.

Berger, A. A. (1997). *Narratives in popular culture, media, and everyday life*. Thousand Oaks, CA: Sage.

Bernstein, B. (1977). *Class, codes and control*. London: Routledge & Kegan Paul.

Bettelheim, B. (1977). *The uses of enchantment: The meaning and importance of fairy tales*. New York: Vintage.

Brenner, C. (1974). *An elementary textbook of psychoanalysis*. Garden City, NY: Doubleday.

Caudwell, C. (1971). *Studies and further studies in a dying culture*. New York: Monthly Review Press.

Culler, J. (1976). *Structuralist poetics: Structuralism, linguistics and the study of literature*. Ithaca, NY: Cornell University Press.

Dichter, E. (1960). *The strategy of desire*. London: Boardman.

Dichter, E. (1964). *Handbook of consumer motivations: The psychology of the world of objects*. New York: McGraw-Hill.

Dressler, D. (1969). *Sociology: The study of human interaction*. New York: Knopf.

Eco, U. (1972, Autumn). Towards a semiotic inquiry into the television message. *Working Papers in Cultural Studies, 3*.

Eco, U. (1976). *A theory of semiotics*. Bloomington: Indiana University Press.

Eidelberg, L. (1968). *The encyclopedia of psychoanalysis*. New York: Macmillan.

Engels, F. (1972). Socialism: Utopian and scientific. In R. C. Tucker (Ed.), *The Marx-Engels reader*. New York: W. W. Norton.

Enzenberger, H. M. (1974). *The consciousness industry: On literature, politics and the media.* New York: Seabury.

Erikson, E. (1968). *Identity, youth, and crisis.* New York: W. W. Norton.

Freud, S. (1962). *Civilization and its discontents.* New York: W. W. Norton.

Freud, S. (1963). *Character and culture* (P. Rieff, Ed.). New York: Collier.

Freud, S. (1965). *The interpretation of dreams* (J. Strachey, Trans.). New York: Avon. (Original work published 1900)

Friedson, E. (1953). Communication research and the concept of the mass. *American Sociological Review, 18*(3).

Frith, S. (1981). *Sound effects: Youth, leisure, and the politics of rock 'n' roll.* New York: Pantheon.

Fromm, E. (1957). *The forgotten language: An introduction to the understanding of dreams, fairy tales and myths.* New York: Grove.

Fromm, E. (1962). *Beyond the chains of illusion: My encounter with Marx and Freud.* New York: Simon & Schuster.

Gitlin, T. (1989, July-August). Postmodernism defined, at last! *Utne Reader,* pp. 52-58, 61.

Glasgow University Media Group. (1980). *More bad news.* London: Routledge & Kegan Paul.

Grotjahn, M. (1966). *Beyond laughter: Humor and the subconscious.* New York: McGraw-Hill.

Haug, W. F. (1986). *Critique of commodity aesthetics: Appearance, sexuality and advertising in capitalist society.* Minneapolis: University of Minnesota Press.

Haug, W. F. (1987). *Commodity aesthetics, ideology, and culture.* New York: International General.

Henderson, J. L. (1968). Ancient myths and modern man. In C. G. Jung with M.-L. von Franz, J. L. Henderson, J. Jacobi, & A. Jaffé, *Man and his symbols* (pp. 104-157). Garden City, NY: Doubleday.

Hinsie, L. E., & Campbell, R. J. (1970). *Psychiatric dictionary.* New York: Oxford University Press.

Horton, P., & Hunt, C. (1972). *Sociology.* New York: McGraw-Hill.

Jakobson, R. (1988). Linguistics and poetics. In D. Lodge (Ed.), *Modern criticism and theory: A reader* (pp. 32-57). New York: Longman.

Jameson, F. (1991). *Postmodernism; or, The cultural logic of late capitalism.* Durham, NC: Duke University Press.

Jones, E. (1949). *Hamlet and Oedipus.* New York: W. W. Norton.

Jung, C. G. (1968). Approaching the unconscious. In C. G. Jung with M.-L. von Franz, J. L. Henderson, J. Jacobi, & A. Jaffé, *Man and his symbols* (pp. 18-103). Garden City, NY: Doubleday.

Katz, E., Blumler, J. G., & Gurevitch, M. (1979). Utilization of mass communication by the individual. In G. Gumpert & R. Cathcart (Eds.), *Inter/media.* New York: Oxford University Press.

Lacan, J. (1966). *Ecrits: A selection* (A. Sheridan, Trans.). New York: W. W. Norton.

Lakoff, G., & Johnson, M. (1980). *Metaphors we live by.* Chicago: University of Chicago Press.

Lazere, D. (1977, April). Article in Mass culture, political consciousness and English studies [Special issue]. *College English, 38.*

Lefebvre, H. (1984). *Everyday life in the modern world.* New Brunswick, NJ: Transaction. (Original work published 1968)

Lesser, S. O. (1957). *Fiction and the unconscious.* Boston: Beacon.

Lévi-Strauss, C. (1967). *Structural anthropology.* Garden City, NY: Doubleday.

Lipset, S. M. (1979). *The first new nation: The United States in historical and comparative perspective* (rev. ed.). New York: W. W. Norton.

Lotman, J. M. (1977). *The structure of the artistic text* (G. Lenhoff & R. Vroon, Trans.). Ann Arbor: Michigan Slavic Contributions.

Lowenthal, L. (1944). Biographies in popular magazines. In P. F. Lazarsfeld & F. Stanton (Eds.), *Radio research 1942-43*. New York: Duell, Sloan & Pearce.

Lyotard, J.-F. (1984). *The postmodern condition: A report on knowledge*. Minneapolis: University of Minnesota Press.

Mandell, A. J. (1974, October). A psychiatric study of professional football. *Saturday Review/World*.

Marx, K. (1964). *Selected writings in sociology and social philosophy* (T. B. Bottomore & M. Rubel, Eds.; T. B. Bottomore, Trans.). New York: McGraw-Hill.

McLuhan, M. (1967). *The mechanical bride: Folklore of industrial man*. Boston: Beacon.

McQuail, D., & Windahl, S. (1993). *Communication models for the study of mass communication* (2nd ed.). New York: Longman.

Messaris, P. (1994). *Visual literacy: Image, mind, and reality*. Boulder, CO: Westview.

Monaco, J. (1977). *How to read a film*. New York: Oxford University Press.

Pines, M. (1982, October 13). How they know what you really mean. *San Francisco Chronicle*.

Propp, V. (1968). *Morphology of the folk tale*. Austin: University of Texas Press. (Original work published 1928)

Real, M. R. (1977). *Mass-mediated culture*. Englewood Cliffs, NJ: Prentice Hall.

Saussure, F. de. (1966). *A course in general linguistics*. New York: McGraw-Hill.

von Franz, M.-L. (1964). The process of individuation. In C. G. Jung with M.-L. von Franz, J. L. Henderson, J. Jacobi, & A. Jaffé, *Man and his symbols* (pp. 158-229). Garden City, NY: Doubleday.

Warner, W. L. (1953). *American life: Dream and reality*. Chicago: University of Chicago Press.

Wildavsky, A. (1989). *Choosing preferences by constructing institutions: A cultural theory of preference formation*. Presidential address delivered at the annual meeting of the American Political Science Association.

Williams, R. (1977). *Marxism and literature*. Oxford: Oxford University Press.

Zeman, J. J. (1977). Peirce's theory of signs. In T. A. Sebeok (Ed.), *A perfusion of signs*. Bloomington: Indiana University Press.

Name Index

Subject Index

About the Author

Arthur Asa Berger is Professor of Broadcast and Electronic Communication Arts at San Francisco State University, where he has taught since
1965. He took early retirement in January 1998 and now teaches only
during the fall semesters. He has published more than 100 articles,
numerous book reviews, and more than 30 books. Among his latest
books are *Essentials of Mass Communication Theory* (1995), *Bloom's Morning: Coffee, Comforters, and the Hidden Meaning of Everyday Life* (1997), *The
Genius of the Jewish Joke* (1997), *Narratives in Popular Culture, Media, and
Everyday Life* (1997), *The Art of Comedy Writing* (1997), and a comic
murder mystery about postmodernism, *Postmortem for a Postmodernist*
(1997). A companion reader to this mystery, titled *The Postmodern*

Presence: Readings on Postmodernism in American Culture and Society, is currently in press. He is now working on two other mysteries: *The Hamlet Case,* which deals with different ways of interpreting Shakespeare's *Hamlet,* and *Murder ad Hominem,* which shows how print advertisements and radio and TV commercials can be analyzed from the perspectives of multiple disciplines.

Dr. Berger is married, has two children, and lives in Mill Valley, California. He has a page on the Internet that includes a list of his books and a number of his articles; his e-mail address is aberger@sfsu.edu.